Buttercream Botanicals
FOR BEGINNERS

Buttercream Botanicals

FOR BEGINNERS

Simple Techniques for Creating Stunning Flowers, Foliage, and More

Leslie Vigil

Brimming with creative inspiration, how-to projects, and useful information to enrich your everyday life, quarto.com is a favorite destination for those pursuing their interests and passions.

First Published in 2022 by Quarry Books, an imprint of The Quarto Group, 100 Cummings Center, Suite 265-D, Beverly, MA 01915, USA. T (978) 282-9590 F (978) 283-2742 Quarto.com

Quarry Books titles are also available at discount for retail, wholesale, promotional, and bulk purchase. For details, contact the Special Sales Manager by email at specialsales@quarto.com or by mail at The Quarto Group, Attn: Special Sales Manager, 100 Cummings Center, Suite 265-D, Beverly, MA 01915, USA.

10 9 8 7 6 5 4 3 2 1

ISBN: 978-0-7603-7612-6

Digital edition published in 2022
eISBN: 978-0-7603-7613-3

Library of Congress Cataloging-in-Publication Data is available.

Design and page layout: Laura McFadden Design, Inc.
Photography: Leslie Vigil

Printed in China

DEDICATION

For Magnolia Jane

Contents

Introduction

IN MY EARLY YEARS OF CAKE DECORATING, I found myself very much in love with all things cake—sculpting, creating structures, crafting fondant details, creating jaw-dropping showpieces, all of it—except buttercream. At the time, buttercream seemed far too limiting, and what I thought I knew about it didn't excite me in the slightest. In fact, I dreaded having to work with buttercream. I didn't want to make humble roses; I wanted to make elaborate, tiered masterpieces with three-dimensional elements such as sugar flowers with hand-painted details. I would soon discover that there was so much more to buttercream than I could have imagined.

Eventually, I grew bored with piping the same flowers over and over again. The typical roses and chrysanthemums were fine, but I began to wonder whether there was something more. What possibilities could there be in creating flowers with buttercream? I longed to create buttercream flowers that were new, more challenging, and more exciting—flowers that would make others rethink the possibilities of buttercream, too. After months of trial and error experimenting with different types of buttercream florals, I discovered a wealth of newfound possibilities was hiding within the basic skills I already knew.

My first attempt at creating buttercream succulents involved many tries to create new techniques that were elaborate and complicated and required two or more piping tips to complete. With all that, the results were still unsuccessful: bulky with too many piped leaves, inevitably resulting in a collapsed pile of buttercream. Once I simplified the process, however, the succulents began to take shape.

Again, I discovered that all the piping skills I needed to create any kind of buttercream botanical—flowers, succulents, leaves, and more—derived from the basic, fundamental skills that I already knew. I named the methods I developed my fundamental four techniques. Starting with these four techniques and incorporating some creative modifications, you'll be able to create more realistic buttercream botanicals.

I've broken down these four techniques in the book, introducing each fundamental method with step-by-step instructions and the essential piping tip needed for best results. Following each fundamental technique are a series of buttercream botanicals that are created with variations of that technique.

I've also shared my signature recipe and method for piping buttercream to help you create these botanicals. My recipe is a hybrid style of buttercream that can be made easily like American-style buttercream but is less sweet and has the lighter texture of a Swiss or an Italian meringue buttercream. This buttercream is a dream, and with its pleasant texture and medium-soft density, you can pipe beautiful buttercream botanicals with ease. Also included are my recipes for vanilla and chocolate cake, a complete checklist for all your tools, and my signature method for creating your very own buttercream botanical cake.

Everything you need to create your own beautiful buttercream botanicals can be found within these pages. Let's get started!

Essential Supplies

When it comes to essential supplies for decorating cakes with buttercream botanicals, there's no need to spend excessively on a collection of high-end equipment and materials. Don't be fooled by gimmicky items with fancy packaging or extra-large decorating kits that claim to contain lots of tools. Whenever possible, I offer inexpensive alternatives for items that can easily be substituted with items you may have on hand. For items that may require more of an investment, I've provided a short, reliable list of online resources (see page 125). Be sure to check out your local cake and candy supply stores for items as well.

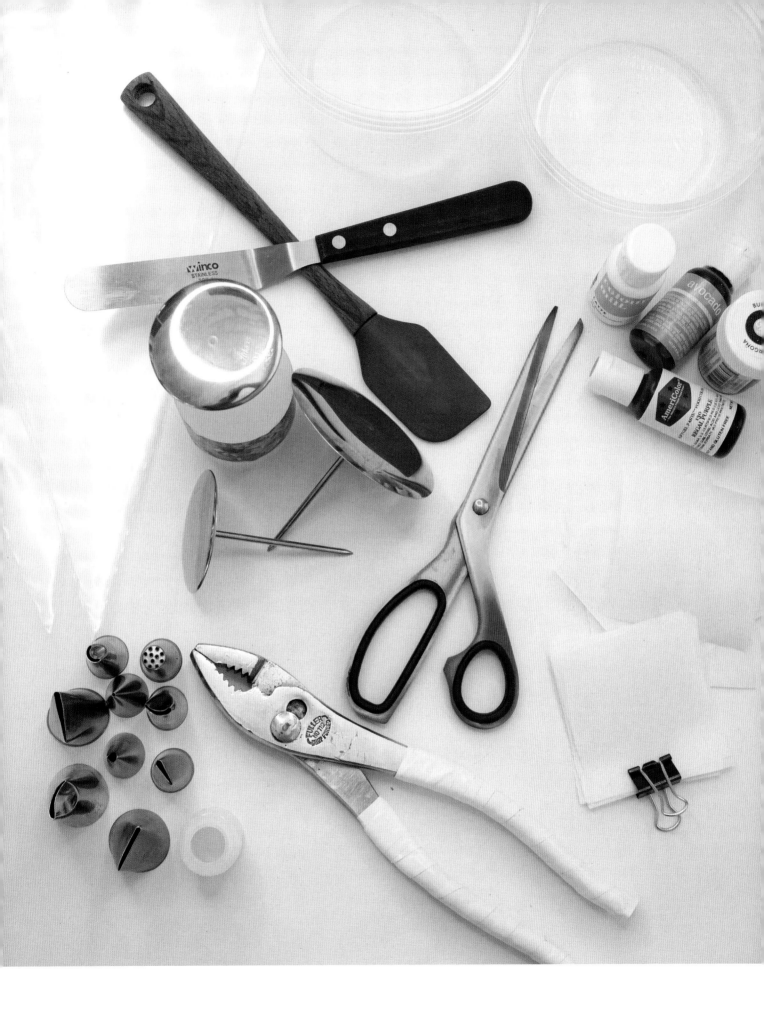

Piping Bags »

A good piping bag (also known as a pastry bag) should be sturdy enough to hold the buttercream but still have enough flexibility to make filling the bag a simple task. For piping botanicals, choose a bag between 12 and 16 inches (30 and 40 cm) in length. I recommend Weetiee and Webake brands.

To fill a piping bag with buttercream, insert the tip of the bag into a tall cup or glass and roll the open end of the piping bag over the sides. Insert the piping tip into the bag and add buttercream to fill, leaving 3 to 4 inches (7.5 to 10 cm) of the top of the bag unfilled. Snip the tip of the piping bag to reveal the piping tip and push the buttercream toward the tip of the bag to remove any air bubbles. Secure the end of the bag with a clamp or rubber band, or twist the bag closed.

Flower Nails »

A flower nail is a handheld tool that provides a flat surface for building buttercream botanicals, and it's available in a variety of sizes and shapes. To use a flower nail for piping, hold the nail portion of the tool in your nondominant hand, rotating it between your fingers as you pipe buttercream onto the head with your dominant hand.

Flower nails are available in plastic or metal (usually stainless steel). Although a plastic nail will work fine, a metal flower nail will last longer. The size of the nailhead you use should be determined by the size of the buttercream botanical you want to create. I recommend working with a nail that's at least 2 inches (5 cm) in diameter; anything smaller will be limiting. The most versatile flower nails are standard nails with flat heads that are 2 or 3 inches (5 or 7.5 cm) in diameter. My favorites are the Ateco 913 (this has a 2-inch [5 cm] diameter head) and the Ateco 914 (this has a 3-inch [7.5 cm] diameter head).

Flower Nail Stand or Block

This accessory isn't an absolute necessity, but it can be useful because it allows you to rest a flower nail in an upright position while piping. These blocks are made from plastic or wood and can be found in square, rectangle, or round shapes. Stands act as a third hand when you need to set the flower nail down. Alternatively, you can use a block of sturdy foam in place of a stand. However, after several uses and perforations from the flower nail, the material will wear down and become less stable and reliable.

Parchment Paper Squares ⌃

Parchment paper squares provide a clean surface for building buttercream botanicals on a flower nail. They also allow you to transfer a completed botanical to a tray for storage. Cut parchment squares to fit the head of the flower nail (2 inches [5 cm] for a 2-inch [5 cm] flower nail, for example), and secure each one to the head of the nail with a dab of buttercream.

Perfectly precise squares aren't necessary, but parchment paper with a printed grid (such as Reynolds Kitchens Parchment Paper with Smart-Grid) is helpful for creating consistent sizes. Any brand of parchment paper will work, and wax paper can be substituted.

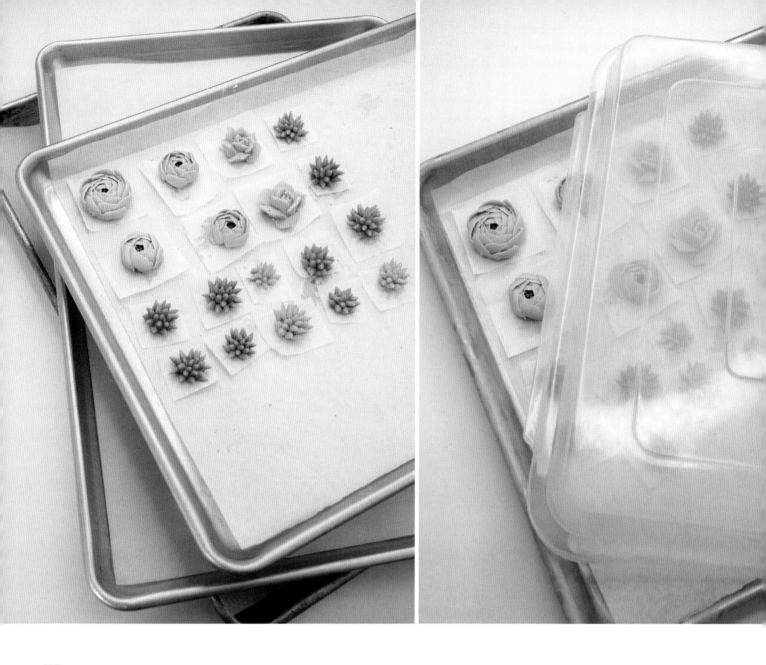

Trays ⌄

Metal sheet trays are necessary supplies for buttercream botanicals. After building botanicals on a flower nail covered with parchment paper, the pieces are carefully transferred to a tray. Trays are placed into the freezer for a minimum of 30 minutes, which allows the buttercream to solidify before being placed onto the cake canvas.

Trays should fit comfortably in the freezer. They come in a variety of sizes, but I prefer metal half sheet baking trays (18 x 13 inches [46 x 33 cm]), also known as jelly roll trays, that have fitted

lids. Metal is a good conductor of temperature, so botanicals will chill thoroughly. Lids allow the trays to be stacked, doubling or tripling the amount of buttercream botanicals that can be stored. These trays also come in quarter sheets (9 x 13 inches [23 x 33 cm]) and full sheets (26 x 18 inches [66 x 46 cm]).

Plastic food storage containers will also work in place of trays. Look for ones that are suitable for freezer storage and are both wide and tall enough to hold botanicals safely.

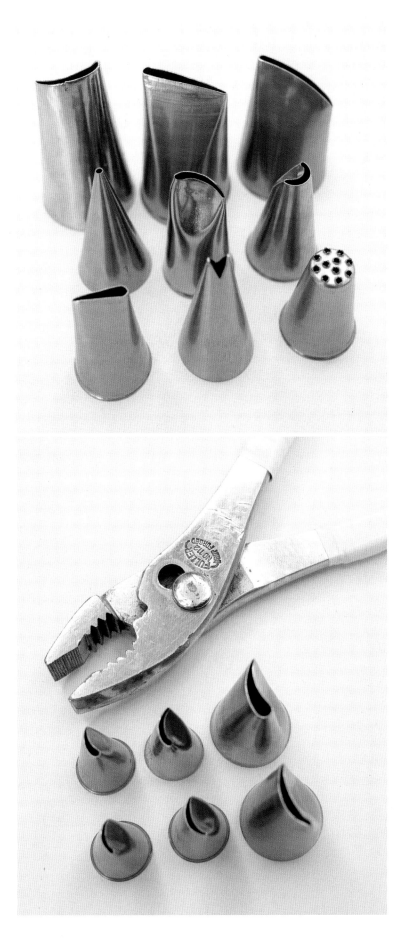

« Piping Tips

Piping tips are metal cone-shaped nozzles with an opening at the narrow end. To use the tip with a piping bag, insert the tip into the narrow end of the bag and fill the bag with buttercream. Cut the tip of the piping bag with scissors to reveal the piping tip.

The shape of the piping tip is where infinite possibilities begin; they can be used to create a wide variety of flower petals, flower centers, leaves, decorative motifs and borders, and much more. With hundreds of shaped tips available, the choices can be overwhelming. Piping tips use numbers to refer to their size and shape. For a detailed breakdown of piping tip categories and deciphering their number labels, see Getting Acquainted with Piping Tips (page 30).

« Slip-Joint Pliers

On occasion, you may need to modify a piping tip. Altering tips changes the way the buttercream is extruded, allowing you to pipe unique shapes that produce more realistic-looking petals. The process involves narrowing the piping tip opening using slip-joint pliers, which can be found at any hardware store. The mouth of the pliers should be flat with dull ridges that can grip the piping tip. To modify a tip, open the pliers and pinch the end of the piping tip to make it more narrow. Do this gradually, applying pressure using pumping motions. Continue pumping with gradual pressure until the desired shape is achieved. (See Modifying Piping Tips, page 34, for more information.)

Gel Colorants »

Gel-based colorants are a must for coloring buttercream. I don't recommend liquid food color that comes in a squeeze pack and is available at the grocery store; that's better suited for other projects. Gel colors are concentrated dyes in gel form that won't dilute or water down buttercream, which keeps the buttercream's structure intact.

To achieve vibrant or saturated colors, add gel color until the desired shade is almost achieved. For lighter colors such as ivory, yellow, or soft pinks, only two to three drops may be needed per cup (8 oz) of buttercream. Certain deep colors such as red, deep purple, or black require larger amounts of gel color. Add approximately ½ teaspoon of gel color per 1 cup (8 oz) of buttercream, but be aware that the buttercream will appear muted or hazy before the color is fully developed. Allow the buttercream to sit at cool room temperature (60°F to 77°F [16°C to 25°C]) for at least 2 hours and a maximum of 24 hours. This time allows the gel color to emulsify into the buttercream and the color to fully develop. Colors intensify with time, so be mindful of the amount of gel color that you add. Adding too much can potentially alter the buttercream's flavor, making it bitter. This is especially true for shades such as red, pink, purple, and black.

If too much gel color has been added, remove some of the colored buttercream and replace it with uncolored buttercream to balance the color and flavor.

Mixing Tools ⌄

Colors can be mixed with buttercream in almost any food-safe container. My go-to vessels for mixing colors are deli containers with lids, which come in various marked sizes that allow me to gauge an estimated quantity of buttercream. One-size-fits-all lids make storing buttercream a breeze. Deli containers can be purchased at any restaurant supply company.

I recommend using small spatulas for mixing buttercream (other utensils will also get the job done). These allow you to simultaneously scrape the sides of the container, blend the buttercream easily and evenly, and efficiently scoop enough buttercream to fill piping bags.

Food Scale ⌃

A food scale is recommended to achieve the most accurate ingredient measurements. Measuring cups are fine to use, but you may experience inconsistent results with the recipes in the book. Food scales measure ingredients by weight and come in various sizes and price ranges, but the most widely available and user-friendly versions are compact and digital.

For the best results, look for a food scale with these features:

- Options for different weight unit measurements such as pounds, ounces, and grams.
- A capacity for at least 11 pounds (5 kg) of ingredients. Some scales on the market have lower capacities, but a scale that can handle more weight is a better investment in the long run.
- A large and clear digital display of measurements.
- A tare or zero button. Use this feature to bring the reading back to zero. This way, you can weigh a bowl or container on the scale before measuring the weight of the ingredients. This is an especially important feature if you're measuring multiple ingredients in the same bowl or container.
- Glass food scales can be fragile, so I suggest opting for plastic or metal.
- Rechargeable food scales are great because batteries don't need to be replaced, but this isn't vital to the functionality of the scale.

Getting Started

In this chapter, I share my signature buttercream recipe and two versatile cake recipes and introduce you to the piping tips and techniques you'll use to make gorgeous buttercream botanicals.

The recipes are easy to follow and yield great results. The piping exercises will prime you for creating botanicals and help you become familiar with holding a piping bag. You'll also discover other basic tools and how to use them. I'll show you some of my methods for developing and customizing color palettes with simple techniques to help you create an array of beautiful colors and take your buttercream botanicals to the next level.

2 pounds (910 g) cold unsalted butter

8 ounces (225 g) pasteurized egg whites, cold

2 pounds (910 g) powdered sugar

1 tablespoon (15 ml) vanilla extract

½ teaspoon salt

Basic Buttercream

Buttercream is the foundation for the flowers, plants, fillers, and designs you'll create, and the recipe can be used to ice cakes as well. Read through the instructions before beginning, make sure your ingredients are prepped, and go over the troubleshooting tips. These tricks will help ensure a perfect batch every time.

Makes 4½ pounds (2 kg) buttercream (about 9 cups)

1 Place the sticks of butter (or 4-ounce portions) in a microwave-safe bowl and microwave on high for about 30 seconds. Rotate the bowl and microwave again for 30 seconds. The butter should be cool to the touch (70°F to 75°F [21°C to 24°C]) and soft and malleable. Pinch the butter with your fingers to test it; it should keep its shape. Set aside.

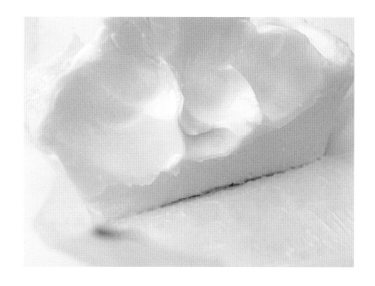

2

3

4

2   In the bowl of stand mixer fitted with a whisk attachment, or with a hand mixer, whip the egg whites and powdered sugar on low until combined. Scrape down the sides of the bowl as necessary. There should be no powdered sugar collected on the sides of the bowl. The mixture will be loose and runny.

3   Whip the mixture on high speed for 5 to 7 minutes, or until it becomes white and glossy. It should be stiff enough to hold a peak briefly when the whisk is dipped into the bowl and pulled out.

4   With the mixer on low speed, gradually add the butter. Once the butter has begun to be incorporated, add the vanilla and salt.

5a

5b

Buttercream Troubleshooting Tips

- For a smooth consistency, switch out the whisk attachment for a paddle after step 5, when the butter has been fully incorporated and no curdling is visible. Then mix on low speed for 10 to 15 minutes to smooth out any large air bubbles.

- To speed up the color development for saturated and vibrant tones, place the buttercream and gel color in a stand mixer fitted with a paddle attachment. Mix on low to medium-low speed until the gel is fully emulsified and the color pops, approximately 5 to 10 minutes (the amount of time may vary). To achieve tints and soft shades with gel color, using a mixer may not be necessary, so simply incorporate the gel color by hand.

- Buttercream may become aerated as it sits. Mix well before using.

- Buttercream will remain stable in an airtight container for 48 hours at cool room temperature, 2 weeks in the refrigerator, and up to 6 months in the freezer.

5 The buttercream may appear broken or curdled shortly after adding the butter (**a**). Continue to mix until fully blended (**b**).

Vanilla Cake

Makes two 8" (20 cm) or three 6" (15 cm) cakes, or two dozen cupcakes

Nonstick cooking spray

2 cups (250 g) all-purpose flour

2½ teaspoons (11½ g) baking powder

¼ teaspoon salt

4 large eggs, at room temperature

1⅓ cups (267 g) granulated sugar

1 cup (235 ml) whole milk

½ cup (112 g) unsalted butter

1 tablespoon (15 ml) vegetable or canola oil

1 tablespoon (15 ml) vanilla extract

SUPPLIES
Stand mixer and one large bowl or a hand mixer and two large bowls or containers, two 8" (20 cm) or three 6" (15 cm) cake pans or two standard cupcake tins (the latter lined with wrappers), parchment paper, a small saucepan, and paperclips (optional)

1   Preheat the oven to 350°F (180°C, or gas mark 4) and prepare the cake pans with nonstick cooking spray (or your preferred pan preparation) and line the bottoms with parchment paper (see Tip below).

2   In a large bowl, sift together the flour, baking powder, and salt and set aside.

tip | Trace the bottom of a cake pan onto a sheet of parchment paper and cut out the circle. Cut multiple circles by folding a large piece of parchment (one fold per cake tin), tracing the cake pan on the top fold, and cutting out all the sheets at once. You can secure the sheets with paperclips to prevent shifting as you cut.

3   Place the eggs and sugar in the bowl of a stand mixer, or in a large bowl if using a hand mixer. Secure the whisk attachment. Combine, gradually increasing the mixer speed to the highest setting and allowing the mixture to whip until almost tripled in volume. The mixture should be light in color, close to white. This should take 7 to 8 minutes.

4   In a saucepan on the stove or in a 16-ounce microwave-safe bowl, heat the milk and butter together until the milk is very hot and the butter is melted. Add the oil and vanilla to the milk mixture and whisk together.

5   Switch the mixer speed to low. Alternately add the dry and wet ingredients to the mixing bowl, beginning with one-third of the dry ingredients and allowing them to incorporate slightly before adding one-third of the wet ingredients. Continue alternating the mixtures, ending with the wet ingredients, until just fully combined.

6   Pour the batter into the prepared pans or lined cupcake tins. Bake the cakes for about 30 minutes and the cupcakes for about 18 minutes, or until the tops of the cakes spring back after touching or a skewer is inserted and comes out clean. Do not overbake. Remove from the oven to cool and store as desired (see Tips below).

tips | Cool the cakes upside down on a cooling rack to flatten any doming that may have developed during baking. This makes for a nice, flat top with little or no need for trimming.

To store the cakes, cover cooled cakes in plastic wrap, wrapping them well. Leave at cool room temperature for no more than 24 hours, in the refrigerator for no more than 3 days, or in the freezer for up to 3 months.

Nonstick cooking spray

2 cups (250 g) all-purpose flour

2 cups (400 g) granulated sugar

¾ cup (65 g) unsweetened cocoa powder

2 teaspoons baking powder

1½ teaspoons baking soda

1 teaspoon salt

1 cup (240 ml) buttermilk or whole milk

½ cup (120 ml) vegetable or canola oil

2 large eggs

2 teaspoons vanilla extract

1 cup (240 ml) hot, strong coffee (See Note on page 26.)

SUPPLIES
Stand mixer and one large bowl, or a hand mixer and two large bowls or containers, two 8" (20 cm) or three 6" (15 cm) cake pans or two standard cupcake tins (the latter lined with wrappers), parchment paper, a small saucepan, and paperclips (optional)

Chocolate Cake

Makes two 8" (20 cm) or three 6" (15 cm) cakes or two dozen cupcakes

1   Preheat the oven to 350°F (180°C, or gas mark 4) and prepare the cake pans with nonstick spray (or your preferred pan preparation) and line the bottoms with parchment (see Tip, page 23).

2 Add the flour, sugar, cocoa, baking powder, baking soda, and salt to the bowl of a stand mixer with a paddle attachment or in a large bowl if using a hand mixer. Briefly mix to combine.

3 In another bowl, combine the buttermilk, oil, eggs, and vanilla and whisk together. Add the buttermilk mixture to the flour mixture and mix on medium speed until fully combined.

4 Reduce the mixer speed to low and gradually add the hot brewed coffee until well combined. The batter will appear runny.

5 Pour the batter into the prepared cake pans or lined cupcake tins. Bake the cakes for about 30 minutes and the cupcakes for about 18 minutes, or until the tops of the cakes spring back after touching or a skewer is inserted and comes out clean. Do not overbake. Remove from the oven to cool and store as desired (see Tip, page 24).

note | Hot brewed coffee perfectly complements the chocolate for an enhanced, slightly more complex chocolate flavor. Choose a medium, dark, or espresso roast coffee for best results.

Working with Color

Achieving a cohesive color palette with buttercream doesn't have to be daunting. The process isn't excessively time consuming and doesn't require a degree in color theory. I suggest starting simply when creating a pleasing color palette, building complexity as you become more confident. Try these techniques to achieve a range of colors for a variety of botanicals.

Gradient Colors

To create a cohesive gradient color palette, choose one shade of gel color. Increasing or decreasing the amount of gel color mixed into separate containers of buttercream results in a beautiful gradient palette.

Add a small amount of gel color to one batch of buttercream and mix thoroughly. Notice the intensity of color you achieve with that amount. If the color is too pale, add more gel color. To achieve light colors, a few drops of color are typically needed, while deeper colors require more gel color to reach their full potential. Remember, colors develop further as they sit.

Mix some of the developed color into another container of buttercream to create a lightened version of the first color. Repeat with the second color batch to create a third, lightest shade. Three shades of buttercream colors make a complete color palette that can be plenty for creating a cohesive arrangement. This same technique can be used for any color. Try it with red for shades of red, coral, and pink, or with hot pink for an array of vibrant and soft pinks. These shades of red, coral, and pink are perfect for just about any flower, but they're particularly lovely for roses, peonies, and dahlias.

Deep and Saturated Colors

To achieve bold, deep colors, the secret is time. Once gel colors have been added to buttercream, allow the buttercream to sit for a few hours at room temperature, 68°F to 75°F (20°F to 24°C). This allows the gel color to emulsify with the buttercream and achieve its ultimate depth and saturation. The technique works wonderfully for creating deep colors such as burgundy, fuchsia, plum, and crimson.

Altering Tones

Bright colors are wonderful and have a youthful feel, but you can create a palette with a more subtle and sophisticated look. Adding a small amount of ivory or brown gel color to a basic buttercream color will tone down the vibrancy.

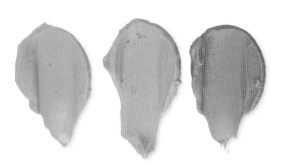

Rose pink (left), rose pink with ivory (middle), rose pink with brown (right)

tip | Be sure to follow proper handling and storage safety measures when leaving buttercream unrefrigerated. Don't allow buttercream to sit at room temperature for longer than 48 hours. See the buttercream recipe (page 20) for further instructions.

Going Green

Green tends to be the most overlooked and undervalued color within the buttercream botanical color palette. Since green often appears in the background of buttercream arrangements as simple leaves, often little consideration goes into selecting a shade of green. Leaf green–colored gels are available, but with some exceptions, they're a tad too bright for my taste when used straight from the bottle. My trade secret for achieving a green shade that complements a palette is to mix a little orange gel color into a prepared green hue. Orange mutes the vibrancy of the blue within the green, making the green more neutral. Try adding a touch of orange to leaf green, forest green, or electric green to achieve more natural shades.

Alternatively, try my favorite shades of green that are perfect straight out of the container. Each of the following greens complements almost any shade of pink, red, or purple botanicals and does not require any alterations:

- Chefmaster: avocado
- Wilton: juniper green and moss green
- AmeriColor: avocado, moss, olive, and cypress

tip

Adding a complementary or near-complementary color will alter other buttercream colors. For example, adding a touch of orange will turn a bright shade of purple into a more muted mauve.

Getting Acquainted with Piping Tips

Becoming familiar with piping tips is key to creating realistic flowers, leaves, and plants. Refer to this overview of essential tips whenever you need a refresher.

Petal Tips »

The opening of the petal tip resembles an elongated teardrop—wide at the base and narrow at the tip—which is perfect for creating flower petals with that shape. These tips have several applications for a variety of techniques but are most commonly used for roses (see Classic Rose, page 63) and blossoms (see Fruit Blossom, page 51). Small petal tips are usually numbered 101 through 104, while medium and large petal tips are numbered 124 through 128.

Among these tips is a range of specialty petal tips that include the letter *K* in the labeled number (see page 35). For example, there is a petal tip 125 and a 125K. Both are petal tips, but the 125K tip has a narrower opening, which produces a thinner petal that mimics petals found in nature and is ideal for creating more lifelike botanicals. Although these specialty petal tips can be a challenge to find, you can modify regular tips with slip-joint pliers (see Modifying Piping Tips, page 34).

Curved Petal Tips ⌃

Like their non-curved counterparts, curved petal tips also produce buttercream petals that are wider at the base and narrower at the tip. However, the curved tip produces a petal with a slight arc.

Depending on how the tip is positioned, curved piping tips can produce petals that curve inward (see Ranunculus, page 68) or outward (see Small Sedum Succulent, page 59). Small curved petal tips are usually numbered 59 to 61, while large curved petal tips are numbered 120 to 123 (see Modifying Piping Tips, page 34, for more information on curved petal tips).

U-Shaped Petal Tips ⌃

U-shaped petal tips bow like curved petal tips but have a much narrower opening that resembles a tiny smile and an even width from end to end. U-shaped petal tip sizes are numbered 79 to 81. These tips are most commonly used for creating chrysanthemums (see page 81) and varieties of aster (see page 85).

« Leaf Tips

Some leaf tips are also referred to as *V*-shaped tips because the opening has a pointed *V* shape. Others have a five-pointed starlike opening. These tips are most commonly used to create simple leaves to fill spaces in floral arrangements. In this book, they're also used to create petals for both flowers and succulents (see Sempervivum Succulent, page 87, and Pomp-Pom Dahlia, page 57). Small *V*-shaped leaf tips are numbered 350 to 352, and the large leaf tip is 353 or 366, depending on the brand. Star-shaped tips are numbered 73 to 76.

« Grass Tips

Grass tips (also known as multi-opening tips) have flat tops and multiple holes for extruding clusters of several buttercream strings at once. These are perfect for creating grass or furlike texture as well as stamens or flower centers (see Ranunculus, page 68). Small tips are numbered 133 or 233, and the large is 234.

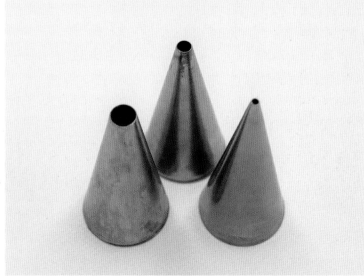

« Round Tips

Round tips are very versatile and are also called plain tips or writing tips. These have various sizes of round openings that can be used for creating fine details on buttercream botanicals, such as stamens, flower centers, and spines on succulents. Numbers range from 0 to 12; 0, 1, 2, and 3 are used most often in this book for creating details.

Couplers ≪

Couplers are two-part tools, consisting of a base and a ring, that allow you to use the same piping bag and swap out the piping tip. The base goes inside the bag and the tip of the bag is cut. The piping tip goes over the base and the bag and the ring twists onto the outside of the piping bag to secure the piping tip. Using a coupler with every piping bag isn't necessary, but it does have benefits.

Using one piping bag and swapping out the tips allows you to use fewer bags when piping the same color of buttercream. A coupler used without a metal piping tip can also double as a large round piping tip (the closest match is an 806 large round tip). The coupler is perfect for piping botanicals such as pine cones because you can use it alone to pipe the base and then attach a piping tip to pipe the scales (see Pine Cone, page 76).

Note that not all piping tips can be used with standard-size couplers because one size doesn't fit all. Standard coupler sets are best suited for smaller piping tips. Medium and large couplers that can be used with larger piping tips are available at some online retailers, but they can sometimes be challenging to find.

For projects in this book, couplers are mostly used for piping bases of buttercream botanicals.

Modifying Piping Tips

When I began piping buttercream botanicals years ago, I never considered modifying my piping tips. But as I gained more experience, I became determined to recreate every kind of botanical I set my eyes on. I quickly realized that to achieve the same thin, ruffled petals of a garden rose or emulate the forms of certain botanicals, I'd need piping tips that looked slightly different from the ones I was using. I loved that a size 127 tip could create a classic rose, but I also needed a tip with a slightly more narrow opening to create petals with a thinner structure and more natural feel. After scouring the internet and baking supply store shelves for petal tips with those exact specifications, I realized I'd have to create them myself. But how?

Enter the slip-joint pliers. This tool allows you to modify piping tips by slightly altering their shape or structure.

To do this, open the mouth of the pliers and pinch the end of the piping tip to make it more narrow. This should be a gradual process, so applying pressure using pumping motions on the pliers is best. Continue pumping with slow, steady pressure until the desired shape is achieved.

The piping tips on the right have been narrowed with slip-joint pliers.

tip | If you squeeze the tip a little too much, making the opening too narrow for buttercream to pass through, correct the mistake by inserting a small, pointed metal spatula into the inside of the piping tip. Wiggle the tip of the spatula back and forth until the opening has widened enough.

The *K* Series Piping Tips ⌃

One series of three petal tips does not require any modifications. These specialty petal tips are referred to as Korean piping tips due to the popularity of the tips in Korea. Korean buttercream flowers are delicate, with multiple layers of thin petals. This style is catching on in other countries, creating a demand for petal piping tips with narrow openings. The labeling of these new piping tips often includes the letter *K* in addition to their numbers. The three Korean-styled piping tips that are now becoming more widely available are labeled 124K, 125K, and 126K.

Getting Started Checklist

One of the most helpful lessons I took away from culinary school was the importance of *mise en place*, a French term that means "putting in place." For a mise en place, necessary tools and components are aligned and ready to go before you begin. Doing so keeps you organized so you can fully focus on the task at hand, setting yourself up for success.

Below is a checklist to help you get started piping your buttercream botanicals, as well as some tips for getting the best results.

- Have all essential supplies on hand: piping bags, flower nails, scissors, parchment squares, trays, piping tips, gel colors, mixing tools, and so on.

- Have a batch of buttercream (or however much you need) prepared and ready to go. If the buttercream has been sitting at cool room temperature for a few hours or even overnight, you may notice that it looks a bit aerated. If so, mix the buttercream with a paddle attachment for a few minutes or mix it by hand. If you're adding gel color, you may find this mixing process does the trick of removing air bubbles and smoothing out the buttercream.

- Have your color palette completed, or nearly completed, before you begin piping the botanicals. You can adjust the colors as you go, if needed, but having them prepared beforehand streamlines the process.

- Before you begin piping the botanicals, have a metal sheet tray nearby or work above the tray to reduce the distance between the flower nail and the tray. This lessens the likelihood of dropping or damaging a flower during the transfer. Make sure the tray fits comfortably in your freezer and there is no risk of an item falling on your beautiful botanicals.

- When piping the botanicals, it's important to remember that variation is key. Don't be too hard on yourself if you think you're not producing flowers or succulents that are identical, and don't fret if every single petal doesn't always fall precisely into place. Variations and flaws occur in nature. Creating buttercream botanicals with these distinctions only adds to the realism. With practice, your skill and control will improve, but as you begin, remember that there is beauty in the differences.

- Once buttercream botanicals are in the freezer, leave them for at least 30 minutes to fully solidify. Larger flowers may require more time, while smaller flowers and leaves may need less. Don't rush the process! Botanicals need to be solid before creating an arrangement on a cake canvas. Too-soft buttercream will cause your flowers to smudge, lose their shape, and/or break during the arranging process, creating a frustrating experience. If you encounter any smudging, return the pieces to the freezer until they're firm enough to handle.

- Buttercream botanicals can be stored in the freezer for a few days, if necessary. If you're storing botanicals for more than a few hours in the freezer, keep the tray covered to prevent air and moisture from seeping in and ice crystals from forming. Any of these can negatively alter the taste and appearance of the buttercream, so be sure to keep them covered with a fitted lid.

- While the pieces are chilling, prepare the cake canvas and stack, fill, and ice the cake (see chapter 5 for inspiration).

- To reduce breakage while arranging the botanicals, try handling them from the base. Any breakage or smudging near the base can easily be concealed when adding final details such as leaves, foliage, filler, and so on.

A Note on Supplies for Buttercream Botanicals

Each of the buttercream botanical lessons requires basic materials that include piping bags, a flower nail and parchment paper square, piping tips, and gel colorant. Because the piping bags, flower nail, and parchment are required for every lesson and don't change, they are not included in the materials lists, but they should be on hand. The specific piping tips and shades of gel colorants are included.

Simple Piping Exercises

Before piping your first complete flower, get comfortable with holding the piping bag. For piping botanicals, a 12- to 14-inch (30 to 35 cm) bag is best. Extra-large bags hold hefty amounts of buttercream that can be heavy and difficult to control. The bag should feel comfortable in your palm, with your fingers resting over the side of the bag. If the bag feels heavy and is straining your wrist, it may be overfilled. Squeeze out some of the buttercream to lighten the weight. If it feels comfortable and manageable now, you're ready for a few easy exercises.

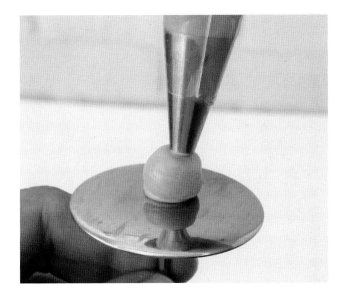

Buttercream Bases

Bases are small mounds or cones piped onto the flower nail that serve as platforms for piping petals. Mound and cone-shaped bases are the most common forms for botanicals that have some volume to them, such as roses and chrysanthemums.

1   Prepare a piping bag with a #10 round tip. Hold the piping bag in your dominant hand and a flower nail in the other. For this exercise, the exact size of the round piping tip isn't vital, but keep in mind that putting more pressure on the bag is required for small piping tips and less pressure is required for larger piping tips.

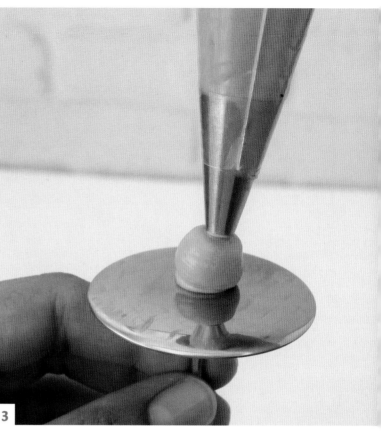

2 To create a cone-shaped base, hover the piping tip just above the surface of the flower nail, about ¼" (6 mm) away, and squeeze out a cone-shaped mound of buttercream. Squeeze firmly at first and then gradually ease and release pressure as you pull upward. This should result in a cone-shaped base. Practice this exercise using different amounts of pressure to create cones that are 1" and 1½" (2.5 and 4 cm) high. Different buttercream botanicals require different size cones.

3 To create a round or mound-shaped base, hover the piping tip just above the surface of the flower nail, about ¼" (6 mm) away, and gradually squeeze the piping bag to form a rounded mound or large pearl. Be sure to completely release pressure on the bag before pulling it away to ensure the mound stays rounded at the top. Practice this exercise using different amounts of pressure to create rounded mounds that are ¼" to 1" (6 mm to 2.5 cm) high. As you practice these exercises a few times, you'll better understand your hand strength and learn how much pressure to apply to the piping bag to achieve the shape and size desired.

1a

1b

2

Spiral Technique

Using two tools at once can feel awkward at first, but with a little practice, such as from this exercise, it will become second nature as your hand-eye coordination improves.

1 Prepare a piping bag with a petal tip, such as #104. Hold the piping bag in your dominant hand and a flower nail in the other. Rest the widest end of the piping tip on the center of the flower nail so the narrow end faces up at a 90-degree angle (**a**). Squeeze the piping bag while simultaneously rotating the flower nail counterclockwise, gradually moving the piping tip outward to create a spiral of buttercream that covers most of the surface (**b**).

2 Maintain even pressure on the bag as you continue to pipe the spiral. This exercise helps you become accustomed to using both tools at once and get familiar with the spiral technique that's used to create buttercream botanicals such as the Classic Rose (see page 63).

1

2a

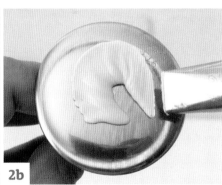
2b

Individual Petals

1 Prepare a piping bag fitted with a petal tip (such as a #104). Hold the piping bag in your dominant hand and a flower nail in the other. Tilt the piping bag so the wide end of the tip touches the center of the flower nail. Squeeze the bag while creating a slight arc, ending back at the center.

2 Create narrow and wide arcs to produce various size petals.

Remember that small petal tips (such as #101, 102, 103, and 104) will create small petals (**a**) while larger petal tips (such as #124, 125, 126, 127, and 128) will create larger petals (**b**).

Adding Color Accents to Botanicals

One of the most striking ways to add depth and realism to your botanicals is with an accent color. By strategically adding a second color to the piping bag with a technique known as striping, you can add yet another interesting element to your buttercream botanicals. Although striping adds an extra step when filling the piping bag, the effort is worth it when you see your finished work.

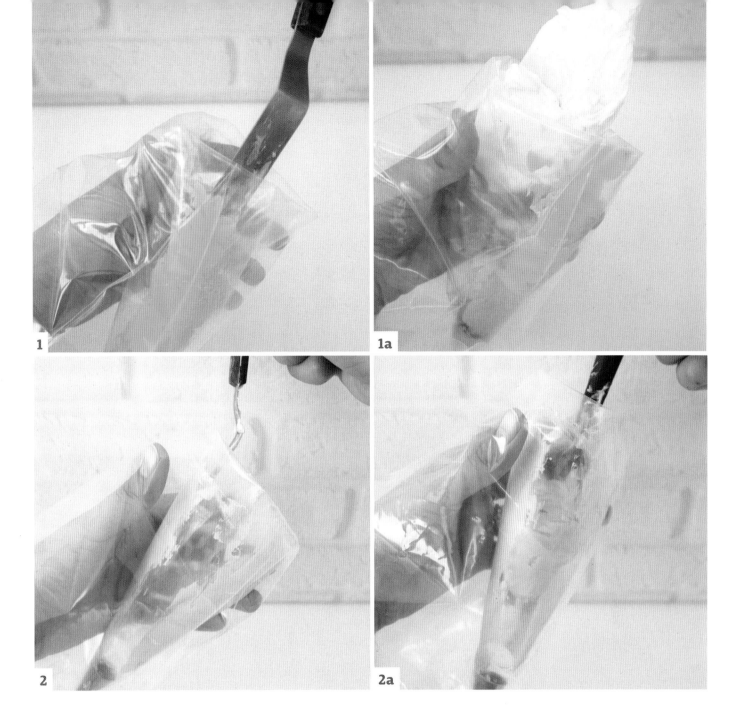

To stripe a piping bag:

1 Prepare the piping bag by inserting a petal tip. Hold the bag open with one hand and use your free hand to smear a stripe of buttercream, starting from the tip of the piping bag (where the piping tip is located) and dragging it along the inside of the piping bag, following the seam of the piping bag as a guide. A small, narrow spatula is the best tool for this. You should have a solid stripe of buttercream established, about 1" (2.5 cm) wide. This will be your accent color.

1a Fill the remaining space of the piping bag with a shade of buttercream that's different from the accent color.

2 For botanicals that require a *U*-shaped piping tip, such as chrysanthemums or agave, add two stripes of color to your piping bag. Each stripe should follow the seams on opposite sides of the piping bag. The end result will be two stripes, about 1" (2.5 cm) wide, along each side.

2a As in step 1a, fill the remainder of the piping bag with a shade of buttercream that's different from the accent color.

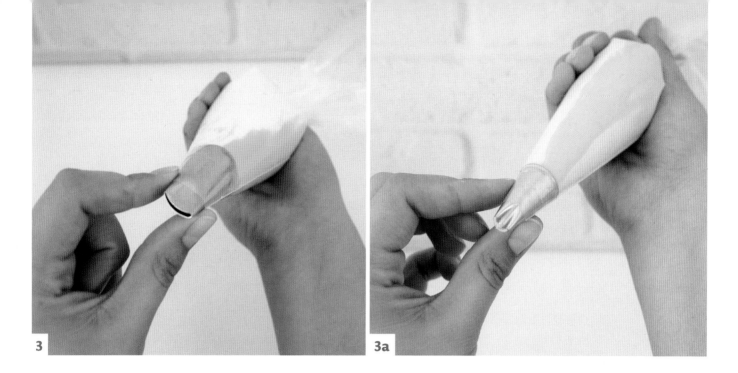

3, 3a Secure the end of the piping bag and then align the piping tip to achieve your desired result.

notes

- For an accent of color on the tips of your petals, align the side of the piping tip that will be producing the tips of the petals. For most petals, such as classic roses and peonies, align the narrow end of the petal tip with the accent color. In the case of echeveria II, align the wide end of the petal tip with the accent color, as that will be the end facing outward.

- For an accent color in the center of the petals, align the side of the piping tip that will be producing the center of the petals. In the case flowers such as fruit blossoms and plumeria, align the wide end of the petal tip with the accent color, as that will be the end facing inward.

- For accent colors with U-shaped piping tips, such as agave succulents and chrysanthemums, follow step 1B. Align the narrow ends of the piping tip with each stripe of color. The accent color will display on the edges of the petals.

Shades of various green
succulents sit atop vanilla
and chocolate cupcakes.

3

The Fundamental Four Techniques

After years of working with buttercream and developing techniques for piping lifelike flowers, succulents, and leaves, I realized that almost every buttercream botanical can be made using one of four techniques. I call them my Fundamental Four Techniques. Mastering these four basic and concise techniques can prepare you to create just about any buttercream botanical you can dream of.

The four techniques are the Blossom Technique, the Rose Technique, the Mum Technique, and the Leaf Technique. In the following sections, you'll learn the techniques along with some variations.

The Blossom Technique is the perfect starting point for any beginner and the basis for a simple yet iconic bloom. The technique is straightforward and highly achievable. As easy as it is, once you learn how to add variations, you'll be amazed at how this little flower can evolve. You'll begin with a nonfussy yet elegant blossom: phlox. Then, you'll play with some piping tips to create the fruit blossom. Make your way to some tropical-inspired plumeria and hibiscus, a fluffy variety of dahlia, and a small succulent called sedum.

Piping tips: petal tip #102 and round tip #1

Gel color (I used AmeriColor Regal Purple for the petals and Wilton Burgundy for the flower center)

Phlox

Phlox are small, five-petal flowers named after the Greek word for fire, due to the brilliant colors of some varieties. The wide range of colors includes white, pale blue, violet, vibrant pink, and deep red. Buttercream phlox can be arranged attractively in clusters on cupcakes and look lovely scattered about as fillers or accents in an arrangement.

You'll imitate the colors of a 'Blue Paradise' phlox, which appears more violet than blue.

1   Prepare two batches of buttercream, one colored with purple and placed in a piping bag fitted with the #102 petal tip and the other colored burgundy and placed in a piping bag fitted with the #1 or #0 round tip (prepare less burgundy buttercream because it will be used for the flower centers only). Place the widest end of the petal piping tip in the center of the flower nail. The piping bag should be almost parallel with the flower nail.

2   Squeeze the piping bag and create a slight buttercream
    arc, ending back at the center. This should produce a
    single petal.

3   Turn the flower nail and reposition the piping bag to the
    starting position in step 2, placing the widest end of the
    petal piping tip at the center. Repeat the arc, creating
    another petal, and return to the center again. This
    second petal should sit beside the first petal.

4   Now that you have two adjoining petals, repeat steps
    2 and 3 and pipe three more petals, for a total of five.

5   Add a center to the phlox. Pipe a small dot of burgundy
    buttercream just outside the middle of the flower. Add
    more tiny dots of buttercream, creating a complete ring
    of color. Leave the center of the flower bare (see the
    finished flower, page 49).

Piping tips: curved petal tip #60 and round tip #1

Gel color (I used Chefmaster Rose Pink for the petals and Chefmaster Golden Yellow for the flower center)

Fruit Blossom

Fruit tree blossoms are one my favorite signs of spring. Blossoms fill once-bare branches with fluffy petals of white or pink, giving the trees such an ethereal feel. For this flower, I took inspiration from the cherry blossom, using a light hand when adding soft pink gel to create the petal color. I used a warm yellow for the stamens in the center of the blossom.

1 Prepare two batches of buttercream, one colored with pink and added to a piping bag fitted with the #60 curved petal tip and the other colored yellow and placed in a piping bag fitted with the #1 round tip (prepare less yellow buttercream because it will be used for the flower centers only).

2 Place the widest end of the curved petal tip in the center of the flower nail. The bag should be almost parallel with the flower nail. Squeeze the piping bag as you create a slight arc, ending back at the center. This will produce a single petal, and you should notice a cupped appearance formed by the curved petal tip.

3 Turn the flower nail and reposition the piping bag to the position you started with in step 2, with the widest end of the piping tip at the center. Repeat the arc and return to the center again. This second petal should sit beside the first petal.

4 Repeat the process and pipe three more petals, for a total of five petals.

5 Add the center accent to the fruit blossom. With the yellow buttercream, gently touch the center of the fruit blossom with the piping tip, squeeze the bag, and pull outward. Repeat until you have a small cluster of pointed stamens that stand upright.

Piping tip: curved petal tip #120

Gel color (I used the buttercream's natural color for the petals and Chefmaster Golden Yellow for the center accent)

Plumeria

Plumeria, also known as frangipani, are native to warm climates and often used in tropical arrangements. These make great filler flowers in buttercream arrangements and can also be a focal component of an arrangement when clustered together. The white and yellow plumeria is the most recognizable, but plumeria blooms can also be found in shades of pink and red with accents of yellow.

1   Prepare the yellow and white buttercreams and use them to fill and stripe a piping bag fitted with the #120 curved petal tip (see page 31). Make sure the widest end of the piping tip is aligned with the yellow buttercream and the narrow end with the white. As in the piping exercises you have practiced, you will start by creating one singular petal. Place the widest end of the piping tip in the center of the flower nail, keeping the bag almost parallel with the nail.

2   Squeeze the piping bag as you create a slight arc, ending back at the center. This should produce one petal with the yellow buttercream on the inside and the white on the outside. These petals will be larger than those of the fruit blossom because this uses a larger piping tip.

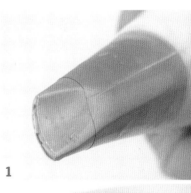

1

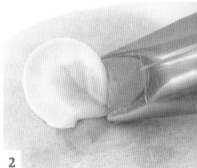

2

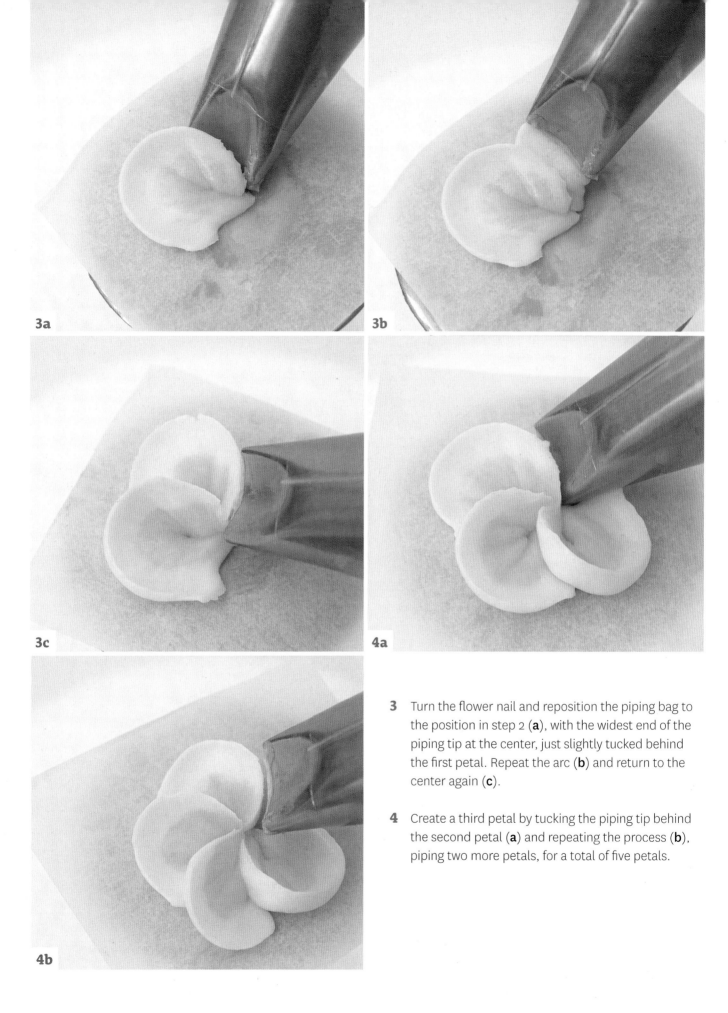

3a

3b

3c

4a

4b

3   Turn the flower nail and reposition the piping bag to the position in step 2 (**a**), with the widest end of the piping tip at the center, just slightly tucked behind the first petal. Repeat the arc (**b**) and return to the center again (**c**).

4   Create a third petal by tucking the piping tip behind the second petal (**a**) and repeating the process (**b**), piping two more petals, for a total of five petals.

Piping tips: large petal tip #127 and round tip #1

Gel color (I used a few drops of Chefmaster Super Red, enough to achieve a nice coral color, and Chefmaster Golden Yellow)

Hibiscus

Hibiscus flowers are an iconic tropical flower that make a great addition to arrangements with a tropical or beachy aesthetic. They can be found in a wide variety of colors, such as yellow, peach, coral, pink, bright pink, red, and white, or with combinations of any of these.

To emulate the ruffled petals, wiggle your wrist during the piping process. This produces petals with a rippled or ruffled appearance.

1 Prepare two batches of buttercream, one colored with red and added to a piping bag fitted with the #127 large petal tip, and the other colored yellow and placed in a piping bag fitted with the #1 tip (prepare less yellow buttercream because it will be used for the flower centers only).

2 Place the widest end of the large petal piping tip in the center of the flower nail, keeping the piping bag almost parallel with the nail.

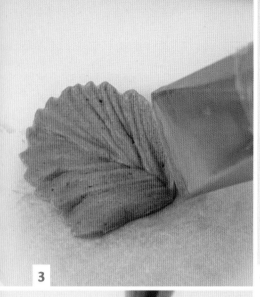

3

4

5

6

3 Squeeze the piping bag, creating a slight arc. Gently wiggle your wrist as you pipe to create a ruffled petal. This wiggling motion will produce a more dimensional petal.

4 Turn the flower nail and reposition the piping bag to the position in step 2, slightly tucking it behind the first petal. Repeat the ruffled arc and return to the center again.

5 Create a third petal by tucking the piping tip behind the second petal and repeating the process, piping three more petals.

6 Create the flower center with the yellow buttercream. Deposit the buttercream in the center of the flower by squeezing the bag and pulling it upward, gradually releasing pressure to create a center that is wide at the base and pointed at the tip.

7 Add tiny stamens to finish by touching the tip of the flower center with the piping tip, squeezing the bag, and pulling outward. Repeat until you have created a few stamens.

7

Piping tip: petal
tip #102

Gel color (I used
Americolor Regal
Purple here, but
dahlias come in an
array of colors so many
other colors will work
as well)

Pompom Dahlia

This variety of dahlia is known as a pompom for its round, fluffy structure. Dahlias are some of the most diverse flowers with hundreds of varieties and come in shades of white, red, pink, orange, yellow, purple, and combinations of these colors. The pompom dahlia is a playful addition to any buttercream arrangement, contributing lots of texture and interest.

1 Prepare a batch of your chosen shade of buttercream and fill a piping bag fitted with the #102 petal tip. Place the widest end of the piping tip in the center of the flower nail with the piping bag parallel with the flower nail.

2 Squeeze the piping bag and turn the flower nail to pipe a ring. This will be a guide to help keep your dahlia round and provide a platform for the petal layers.

2

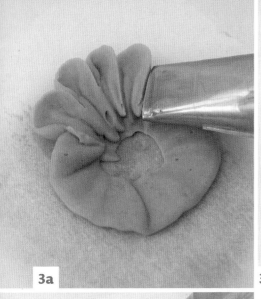

3a

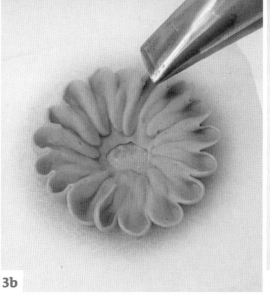

3b

5

6

3   Starting on the outside of the ring, pipe a circle of short, arced petals, using the same technique as with the previous petals (**a**). Repeat several times to produce a complete circle, creating the first layer of petals (**b**).

4   Turn the flower nail and reposition the piping bag as in step 1, with the widest end of the piping tip at the center of the petal ring.

5   Repeat step 3, creating another set of petals on top of the first.

Make the petal arcs shorter to produce a smaller, more narrow petal. Complete another ring of petals.

6   Continue making layers of ringed petals until there are a total of four or five layers, with each layer being slightly smaller than the previous one to produce a domelike shape.

7   To finish the dahlia, deposit five to six small petals in the center.

7

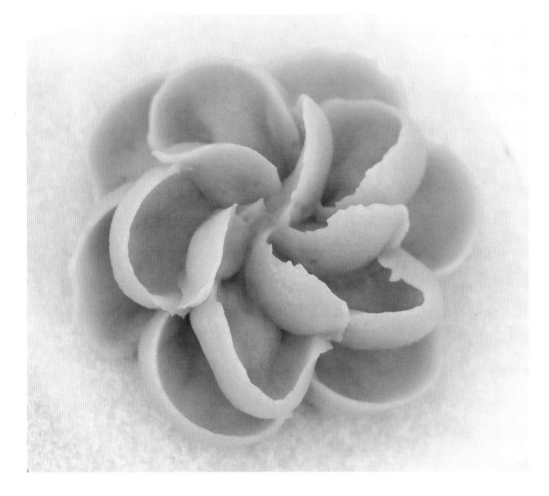

Piping tip: curved petal tip #60

Gel color (I used Chefmaster Avocado)

Small Sedum Succulent

Sedum, also known as stonecrop, are a classification of small, compact succulents that grow in clusters. These plants can be found in various shades of green, silvery blue, and yellow, sometimes with pops of color such as purple, pink, and deep maroon. Because of their small size, sedum make great additions to any buttercream arrangement as fillers.

1   Prepare a batch of buttercream colored a soft green. Fit a piping bag with the curved petal tip #60 and fill it with the buttercream. Place the widest end of the piping tip in the center of the flower nail with the piping bag almost parallel to the nail.

2   Squeeze the piping bag to create a slight arc, ending back at the center. Make this leaf slightly more narrow than in the previous lessons because this botanical requires six petals.

3   Turn the flower nail and reposition the piping bag as in step 1. Make another buttercream arc and return to the center again.

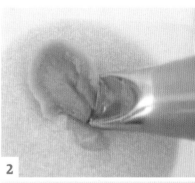

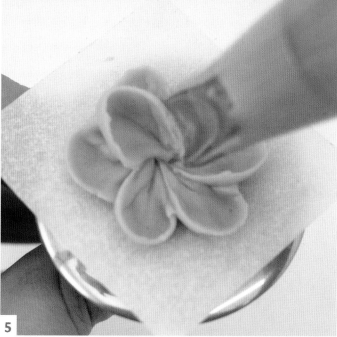

4 Repeat steps 2 and 3 and pipe four more leaves.

5 Create another ring of leaves as you did in steps 2 through 4, layering it on top of the first ring. Start this ring between two of the leaves from the first layer and make the arc shorter to produce a smaller, narrower leaf.

6 Repeat steps 2 through 4 until you have a complete second set of leaves on top. Note that there may be space for five leaves instead of six.

7 Complete the succulent by tilting the piping bag upright at a 90-degree angle. Deposit a petal of buttercream with a gentle squeeze, then pull upward and away to create a short, narrow petal.

8 Repeat step 7 until you have completed three to six more of these petals to finish the succulent (see finished succulent, page 59).

A cupcake goes bold and tropical
with a coral-colored hibiscus and
a few basic leaves.

Roses are classic, elegant, and timeless beauties. The rose form is unmistakable and symbolizes love and romance. In nature, roses bloom in a rainbow of colors and varieties, making them some of the most inspired flowers to recreate. The rose technique is an absolute must to learn and an essential skill for any buttercream artist.

This method is the foundation for creating eye-catching variations of buttercream botanicals, including the classic rose's ruffled counterpart, the garden rose. Other flowers and plants derived from this method are the peony, ranunculus, echeveria succulents, and pine cone.

Piping tip: petal tip
#125K or #125

Note: For smaller
versions of the classic
rose, use a petal tip
#104; for larger ones,
use a petal tip #127.

Gel color (I used Wilton
gel paste in Burgundy,
just enough to achieve a
rich pink)

Classic Rose

The rose is arguably the most recognizable and universal flower. This classic rose technique creates a flower with a defined and spiraled center surrounded by unfurling petals, with an eye toward simplicity. Rather than piping unlimited petals and ultimately losing the rose's definition, this simplified approach creates a numbered sequence of petals that keeps the overall structure defined while maintaining the integrity of the rose.

1 Prepare a batch of burgundy colored buttercream. Fit a piping bag with the #125K or #125 petal tip and fill it with the buttercream.

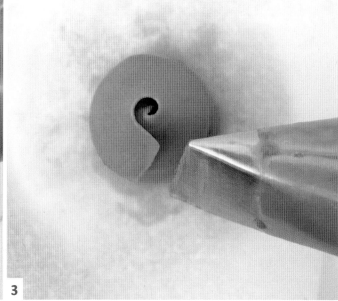

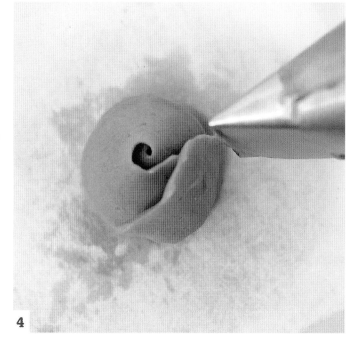

2 Create a cone-shaped base on the flower nail. Hold the piping bag at a 45-degree angle, squeeze firmly, then gradually release pressure and pull upward to create a conelike shape that is wide at the base and narrow at the top. The base should be no larger than ½" (1.3 cm) high. A taller base will result in a top-heavy structure that will be difficult to control, leading to the flower toppling over midway through the process. Every petal will sit on this base, which will give the flower its shape and the impression of it opening or unfurling.

3 Starting near the top of the cone-shaped base, squeeze the piping bag, rotate the flower nail, and wrap a ribbon of buttercream around the top. This is the center of the rose, and it should look like a spiral. If the center appears to lack definition, wrap another ribbon again until a spiral is achieved.

4 Begin the first sequence of petals. Create a single arced petal that takes up no more than one-third of the space around the spiraled center.

tip | If the flower starts to feel top-heavy after step 3, wrap a ribbon of buttercream around the bottom of the base to reinforce the structure.

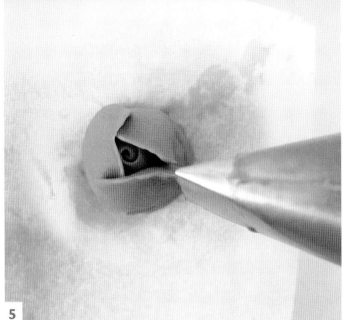

5

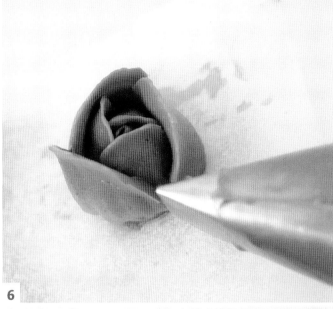

6

7

8

5 Make two more petals the same way. Viewing the rose from the top it should appear triangular, not round, and the center spiral should be clearly visible.

6 Pipe a second layer of arced petals, this time angling your piping bag outward slightly to create three more slightly overlapping petals. This set of petals should be offset from the first so the petals aren't layered on top of each other.

7 Repeat step 6, this time creating five petals and angling the piping bag even farther outward. This angle should be almost parallel with the flower nail. If the petals are

flopping over, remove them and apply firmer pressure while piping the rose petals. Using firmer pressure deposits more buttercream, making the petals a little thicker and with a stronger structure. Make sure the new petals come in contact with the base or previously piped petals so they're stable.

8 Repeat step 7 with a second set of five petals. Note that as you go, you'll need to angle the piping tip even farther outward, until it's almost parallel with the flower nail. As an option, add a third set of five petals for a larger, voluminous rose (see the finished rose, page 63).

Piping tip: curved petal tip #120

Note: For peonies with extreme volume and size, use a curved petal tip #123.

Gel color (I used Chefmaster Rose Pink for the petals and uncolored buttercream to add an accent to the edges)

Peony

The peony is a glorious and showy flower. Peonies are much like roses in their structure but with amplified volume and a striking presence. Peonies begin with tight overlapping petals and gradually expand to reveal their voluminous, ruffled form. These are great standalone flowers, so a single peony can be added to any arrangement as a focal point or to showcase alone. They also collaborate well with other ruffled flowers such as garden roses or botanicals with a contrasting structure such as echeveria and ranunculus. You'll use a curved petal tip for this flower, which allows the petal and overall shape to form organically.

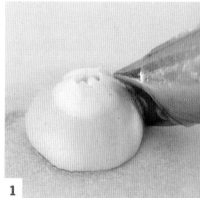

1

1 Prepare a batch of colored buttercream. Fit the piping bag with the piping tip and fill it with the buttercream. Pipe a mounded base on the flower nail (see page 12). Squeeze the piping bag and rotate the flower nail to create the mound. This will serve as the majority of the peony's volume.

2 Starting from the top of the mound, tilt the piping tip inward and pipe a short, arced petal, allowing the petal to rest against the mound.

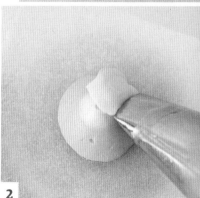

2

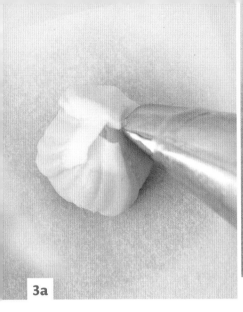

3a

3b

4

3 Repeat step 2, creating more short, arced petals. Allow each to overlap and continue all the way around the mound until you've piped three or four rows of petals (**a**). Keep the piping tip angled inward as you go. The center of the peony should look very similar to a tight ranunculus (**b**) (see page 68).

4 To create the middle petals of the peony, angle the piping tip slightly outward. Pipe an arced petal (similar to the classic rose, page 63), but jiggle your wrist as you pipe to produce a ruffled petal. This petal should take up approximately one-fifth of the outer perimeter, and the inner mound of petals should still be clearly visible.

5 Repeat step 4, creating a total of five ruffled petals surrounding the inner mound of tight petals.

6 Repeat step 5, piping another five ruffled petals and angling the piping tip even farther outward. The gradual angling of the piping tip is vital to the shape of the peony, helping it resemble the flower in bloom.

7 Repeat step 6 and continue adding three to four more outer layers of petals (see the finished flower, page 66). As you pipe, angle the piping tip even farther outward, until it is almost parallel with the flower nail, to create the petal shapes. If the petals flop over, remove them and apply firmer pressure while re-piping the petals. The new petals should touch the base or previously piped petals so they're stable.

5

6

Piping tips: large grass tip (Ateco #234 or Wilton #233), curved petal tip #61, and small round tip #3

Note: A curved petal tip #60 can be used to create smaller flowers, and a curved petal tip #120 can be used for larger ones.

Gel color (I used Chefmaster Liqua-Gel Avocado for the center, Wilton Burgundy for the petals, and Wilton Juniper for the center accent)

Ranunculus

The ranunculus, also known as buttercup, is a bloom with tightly packed petals and a charming, round shape. These flowers can be found in shades of cream, pale yellow, peach, vibrant pink, orange, and purple. The ranunculus complements almost any flower in an arrangement and pairs perfectly with roses, peonies, and dahlias.

Making the ranunculus requires three different piping tips: A large grass tip forms the textured base, a small round tip is used for the center accent, and a curved petal tip creates the flower's rounded form.

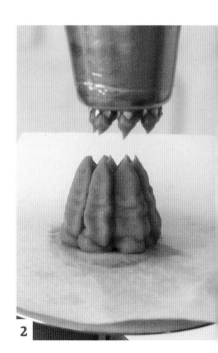

1 Prepare batches of colored buttercreams. Fit one piping bag with the grass tip and fill it with the avocado buttercream, fit another with the curved petal tip and fill it with the burgundy buttercream, and fit another with the round tip and fill it with the juniper buttercream.

2 Create the flower base upon which the petals will be built. Using the piping bag with the grass tip, pipe a small mound of buttercream on the flower nail.

3

4

5

3   Build the flower center. Position the curved piping tip so the wide end is touching the flower nail and the narrow end faces upward. Squeeze the piping bag while simultaneously rotating the flower nail counterclockwise to wrap the base in a ribbon of buttercream. This serves as a barrier to prevent the next layers of petals from collapsing over the base and eclipsing the base color, as a little of that color should peek through.

4   Begin piping the first layer of six petals. Squeeze the piping bag, arcing the tip as you make a single petal to cover about one-third of the center. Allow the petal to rest on the center. To pipe the second petal, begin at the middle portion of the first petal, repeating the same arced motion to create a similar petal that overlaps the first.

5   Repeat step 4 for the remaining four petals until the first layer of ranunculus petals wraps completely around the center. For this portion, the sixth petal can meet with the edge of the first petal or overlap it. Because you'll be adding outer petals, the juncture doesn't have to be precise.

tip | Ranunculus centers are often green. Here, I opted for a medium shade of green to enhance the burgundy of the petals. When creating a lighter or softer shade of ranunculus, such as peach, a lighter shade of green is appropriate for a natural appearance.

6

6 Create a second layer of petals, repeating the arcing motions and overlapping petals from steps 4 and 5. This time, however, create seven petals with slightly wider arcs than the first set. Making wider petals is necessary because they're layered on the base, the center, and the first set of petals.

7 Repeat the petal sequence once more, this time creating a layer of eight slightly wider petals that wrap around the second layer. For this outer portion, the eighth petal should overlap the first petal of this sequence.

8 To create a larger ranunculus, continue the overlapping petal sequence, adding nine petals (see the finished flower, page 68). The overall size of the ranunculus should not exceed 1¾" (4.5 cm) in diameter.

9 When the ranunculus form is complete, add final touches to the center. Using juniper buttercream and the small round piping tip, pipe a slightly oblong pearl in the center of the flower, leaving as much of the base color showing as possible. This accent should emulate the button detail of an actual ranunculus, not fill the center of the flower (see the finished flower, page 68).

Gel color (I used Chefmaster Avocado)

Echeveria Succulent I

Succulents have made their way into the botanical buttercream arena in recent years. These plants add an unexpected, playful yet sophisticated element to any arrangement. Most succulents come in shades of green creating beautiful compositions on their own. They also fit in nicely with any grouping.

This echeveria succulent I has a similar structure to the classic rose and even uses the same petal tip.

1   Prepare a batch of colored buttercream. Fit a piping bag with the #125 tip and the buttercream. Create a cone-shaped base on the flower nail. This base is where all the leaves of the echeveria will sit to create the succulent's shape that gives the impression of "opening" or "unfurling." Hold the piping bag at a 90-degree angle, squeeze firmly, and then gradually taper off the pressure and pull upward to create a conelike shape that is wide at the base and narrow at the top. This base should not exceed a height of ½" (1.3 cm). Too tall of a base will result in a top-heavy structure that will be difficult to control, leading to the succulent toppling over midway through the process.

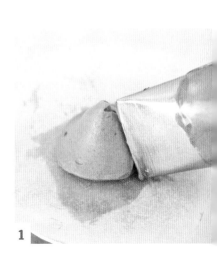

1

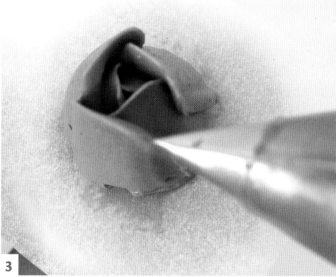

2 Begin the first sequence of leaves. Create a single arced leaf that takes up no more than one-third of the space around the base. Repeat to create a total of three leaves that slightly overlap each other.

3 For the second sequence of leaves, repeat the arced leaves, this time angling the piping bag outward slightly, to create a total of six slightly overlapping leaves.

4 Repeat the process once more with a sequence of six leaves, angling the piping bag even farther outward. This angle should be almost parallel with the flower nail. If you find the leaves flopping over, remove the fallen ones and apply a firmer pressure while repiping them. Make sure the new leaves come in contact with the base or existing leaves so they're stable.

5 If more volume is desired, pipe a third set of six leaves.

Piping tip: petal tip #125

Note: For a mini echeveria succulent II, use a #104 tip; for a larger plant, use a #127 tip.

Gel color (I used Chefmaster Avocado and striped the bag with Americolor Ivory)

Echeveria Succulent II

This echeveria variation is one of my signature buttercream botanicals. It is similar to its counterpart on page 71 but with an innovative twist in technique. Just a few simple adjustments make this version one of the most realistic and eye-catching buttercream succulents. These botanicals look great in single shades of green, but adding an accent color for the tips makes for an elevated presence.

Unlike with the first echeveria technique, you'll flip the piping tip and use the widest part of the tip to create leaves that are thicker in appearance. This small trick gives the leaves a unique look.

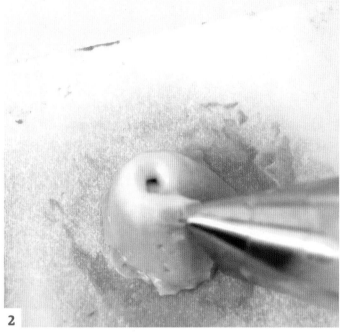

2

3

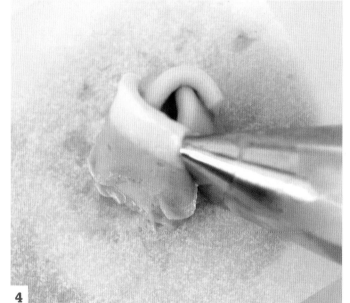

4

1   Prepare batches of green and ivory colored buttercreams. Fit a piping bag with a #125 tip and fill and stripe the piping bag with the two buttercreams (see page 43).

2   Create a cone-shaped base on the flower nail (see page 39). This base is where all the leaves of the succulent will sit to create a shape that gives the impression of opening. Hold the piping bag at a 90-degree angle, squeeze firmly, and then gradually taper off the pressure and pull upward to create a conelike shape that's wide at the base and narrow at the top. The base shouldn't be higher than ½" (1.3 cm). If the base is too tall, the structure will be top-heavy and difficult to control, and the succulent may collapse during the process.

3   To create the first series of leaves, position the piping tip so the widest end faces outward and the ivory color is on top. This will create thicker leaves than the ones you created for the echeveria succulent I (page 71). Pipe a single arced leaf that takes up no more than one-third of the area around the base.

4   Repeat step 3 to create a total of three leaves that slightly overlap each other.

5   Repeat the series of three more leaves, staggering their placement.

6   Repeat steps 3 and 4 to create a third layer of arced leaves, but this time angle the piping bag outward slightly and pipe five slightly overlapping leaves.

7   Pipe one to two more sequences of five petals, angling the piping bag even farther outward. This angle should be almost parallel with the flower nail. If some of the leaves flop over, remove them and apply firmer pressure while piping the leaves. Make sure the new leaves are touching the base of the existing leaves so they're stable.

8   To finish the succulent, use your index finger to tap the outer edge of each petal, then gently flick it outward. This creates a pointed edge for each leaf of the succulent, creating a realistic look. You may use your pinky finger for the smaller succulent leaves.

Piping tips: large round tip #806 (or a coupler without the ring attachment; see page 33) and a small curved petal tip #60 or #61

Gel color (I used Americolor Chocolate Brown)

Pine Cone

Pine cones are wonderful fall and winter botanicals that are perfect to display on their own in a variety of sizes or accompanied by other seasonal botanicals. Try pairing pine cones with sunflowers for an autumnal arrangement or with poinsettias and holly for a festive winter holiday bouquet.

To create a pine cone, you'll use two piping tips: one for the base and the other to pipe the scales, those petal-like elements attached to the center.

1 Prepare a batch of colored buttercream. Fit one piping bag with a large round tip (or coupler without the ring attachment) and another with a small, curved petal tip and fill both with the buttercream.

2 On a flower nail, create a cone-shaped base on which the scales will sit to create the pine cone's signature form

(see page 40). Hold the round-tip piping bag at a 90-degree angle, squeeze firmly, and gradually taper off pressure and pull upward to create a conelike shape that's wide at the base and narrow at the top. The base should not be higher than 1½" (4 cm). A base that's too tall creates a top-heavy structure that may cause the pine cone to fall during the piping process.

2

3

4

5

3 Switch to the curved petal tip piping bag. With the narrow end facing straight up, pipe a single narrow scale at the very tip of the base. There is no need to use an arced motion this time as we are only creating a narrow width; the curvature of the petal tip creates the shape for us.

4 Holding the bag at a 90-degree angle, move slightly down the base and pipe three scales that surround and support the single scale. The first scale should still be longer than the three right below it.

5 Move down the cone-shaped base again and pipe five arced scales that surround the previous ring.

Be sure to stagger placement of these five scales so the previous set of scales is visible.

6 Continue moving down the base, piping rows of narrow scales and staggering their placement until the mound is covered in scales and resembles a pine cone. You will probably need four or five additional rows to almost complete the shape.

7 For the final bottom row of scales, hold the piping bag at a 10- to 20-degree angle to complete the pine cone shape.

6

7

This cake is iced in soft pink with a horizontal texture (see page 108) and is paired with deep pink classic roses, flower buds, leaves, and nonpareils.

A festive stitched cake is adorned with pine cones, hellebores, and icy sugar snow.

Chrysanthemums (or mums) are a somewhat underrated flower, often overlooked and regarded as common. But mums are incredibly versatile, blooming in an array of colors and easily adapted to fit any arrangement regardless of season or occasion. Their unique petal structure sets them apart from blossoms or roses, making their shape and texture the perfect element for adding depth and variation to any grouping. The mum technique also produces other multi-petaled and textured buttercream botanicals, including sunflowers, asters, a variety of succulents, and poinsettias.

Piping tip: *U*-shaped petal tip #80

Note: To create smaller mums, use a #81 tip.

Gel color (I used Chefmaster Neon Brite Purple)

Chrysanthemum

With their compact, abundant petals and unique texture, chrysanthemums are great additions to arrangements that include botanicals that incorporate the blossom and rose techniques. The size is easily modified by adjusting the dimensions of the base. Chrysanthemums require *U*-shaped petal tips to achieve the right width and curvature.

1   Prepare a batch of colored buttercream. Fit a piping bag with a #80 tip and fill it with the buttercream.

2   Create a spiral base on the flower nail (see the spiral technique, page 41). Place the piping tip in the center of the flower nail while keeping the bag parallel to the nail and rotate the nail while simultaneously squeezing the piping bag, creating a spiral of buttercream. Pipe a spiraled base of about ½" (1.3 cm) in diameter.

2

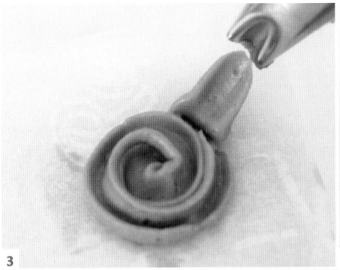

3 Hold the piping bag at a 10- to 20-degree angle from the flower nail with the *U*-shaped tip facing upward. Touch the piping tip against the outermost part of the spiral base and squeeze one petal onto the base. Apply pressure and gently pull the tip away, gradually releasing pressure and staying at a 10- to 20-degree angle.

4 Shift the piping tip so it's next to the first petal and repeat step 3, piping elongated petals around the perimeter of the base.

5 Pipe another row of petals on top of the first set, starting slightly inward from the first row and releasing pressure at a 30- to 40-degree angle from the flower nail. Beginning with this second row, the number of petals will begin to decrease.

6 Pipe a third tier of petals, this time releasing pressure while holding the bag at a 50- to 60-degree angle.

7 Fill the flower center with two to four petals, holding the bag at a 70- to 80-degree angle from the flower nail to round out and complete the shape of the chrysanthemum (see the finished flower, page 81).

Piping tips: leaf tip #74 and star tip #18

Gel color (I used Chefmaster Golden Yellow and Chefmaster Buckeye Brown)

Sunflower

With their large, textured centers and petals in shades of warm yellow, sunflowers are an expressive sign of late summer and autumn. Sunflowers are larger than some buttercream botanicals, so they work well as the focal point of an arrangement along with other autumnal accents, such as autumn leaves (see page 97) and branches (see page 118).

1   Prepare batches of yellow and brown buttercreams. Fit one piping bag with the leaf tip and fill it with the yellow buttercream and fit the other with the star tip and fill it with the brown buttercream.

2   Create a spiral base on the flower nail (see page 41). Holding the bag parallel to the flower nail, place the leaf tip at the center of the flower nail and rotate

it while simultaneously squeezing the piping bag. Pipe a tight spiral base that's about 1" (2.5 cm) in diameter.

3   Starting from the outer perimeter of the base, touch the leaf tip against the base and squeeze one petal onto the base. Apply pressure to the piping bag and gently pull the tip away, gradually releasing pressure at a 0-degree angle to allow the petal to lie flat against the flower nail.

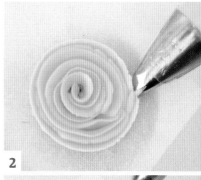

2

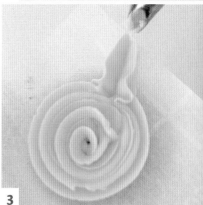

3

4   Shift the piping tip so it's next to the first petal and repeat step 3.

5   Continue piping petals around the perimeter of the base.

6   Pipe a second row of petals on top of the first set, making sure to start slightly inward from the first row and releasing pressure on the bag while holding it at a 10- to 20-degree angle. The second row should have fewer petals than the first row.

7   Create the flower center using the piping bag fitted with the star tip and brown buttercream. Start from the outermost section of the center spiral and squeeze the piping bag to deposit a slightly flattened buttercream star. Follow the shape of the center to create a ring of stars.

8   Fill in the ring by placing more stars evenly in the center until it's filled (see the finished flower, page 83).

Piping tips: *U*-shaped petal tip #81 and small round tip #1

Gel color (I used Americolor Regal Purple and added Americolor Royal Blue to deepen the shade. I also used Chefmaster Gold for the centers.)

Aster

Asters have a similar structure to chrysanthemums but feature open centers displaying contrasting stamens. Compact in size, but often very bold in color, asters are beautiful additions to compositions containing chrysanthemums or displays that need accents of texture and vivid color.

1   Prepare batches of purple and blue buttercreams. Fit one piping bag with the *U*-shaped petal tip and fill it with the purple buttercream. Fit another piping bag with the small round #1 tip and fill it with the blue buttercream.

2   With the *U*-shaped tip, create a spiral base on the flower nail (see page 41). Hold the piping bag parallel to the flower nail and place the piping tip in the center of the flower nail and rotate while simultaneously squeezing the piping bag to pipe a base about ½" (1.3 cm) in diameter.

2

3

4

5

6

3 Starting from the outer perimeter of the base, touch the piping tip against the base and squeeze one petal onto the base. Apply pressure and gently pull the piping bag away, gradually releasing pressure while holding the bag at a 10- to 20-degree angle.

4 Move the piping tip next to the first petal and repeat step 3, piping elongated petals around the perimeter of the base.

5 Pipe a second row of petals on top of the first set, starting slightly inside the first row and releasing pressure on the piping bag while holding it at 30- to 40-degree angle. The second row should have fewer petals than the first row.

6 Pipe a third ring of petals, this time releasing pressure on the bag while holding it at a 50- to 60-degree angle.

7 To create the center stamens of the aster, use the bag fitted with the #1 tip. Place the tip in the center and squeeze while pulling upward to produce a single strand of icing. Repeat until the center is filled in.

7

Piping tip: leaf tip #352

Gel color (I used Wilton gel paste in Juniper)

Sempervivum Succulent

Sempervivums are varieties of succulents with compact, pointed tips. Also known as semps and hens and chicks, these spiny succulents offer a distinctive texture to an arrangement. They pair well with other succulents or with any mixture of botanicals.

1 Prepare a batch of colored buttercream. Fit a piping bag with the leaf tip and fill it with the buttercream. Create a spiral base on the flower nail (see page 41). Hold the piping bag parallel to the flower nail and place the tip at the center of the flower nail and rotate the nail while squeezing the piping bag. Pipe a base about ½" (1.3 cm) in diameter.

2 With the piping bag held at a 90-degree angle to the flower nail, pipe a single leaf at the center tip of the base. Squeeze the piping bag and pull upward, gradually tapering off the pressure. This will produce a single leaflike shape that stands upright.

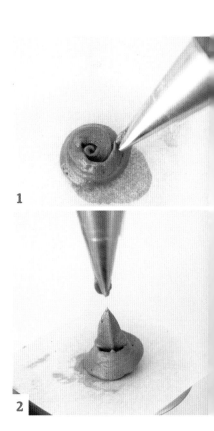

3

4

5

6

3 While continuing to hold the piping bag at a 90-degree angle, pipe three leaves to surround (and support) the single leaf. The first leaf should be longer than the other leaves.

4 Move the piping tip out from the existing group of leaves and pipe five narrow leaves that surround the existing leaves, holding the piping bag at a 60- to 70-degree angle.

5 Move down the base, piping rows of narrow leaves and staggering them so one is not directly behind another. Continue piping until the base is surrounded with leaves. You will likely need four or five rows of leaves to almost complete the shape.

6 Pipe the final bottom row of leaves while holding the piping bag at a 10- to 20-degree angle to complete the sempervivum shape.

Piping tip: *U*-shaped tip #80

Gel color (I used Chefmaster Sky Blue tinted with a hint of Chefmaster Coal Black)

Agave Succulent

Agave plants are a large variety of succulent, with rows of upward-facing leaves. Their colors are often subdued shades of green or silvery blue, sometimes variegated or accented with shades of ivory or soft yellow along the leaves. The structure of this agave incorporates the piping techniques of a chrysanthemum (see page 81). By using a two-toned buttercream, you'll create soft, silvery blue leaves accented with ivory on the outer edges to mimic the look of a variegated blue agave.

1 Prepare batches of blue and black buttercreams. Fit a piping bag with the *U*-shaped tip. Fill and stripe the piping bag with the two shades of buttercream (see page 43).

2 Create a spiraled base on the flower nail (see page 41). Hold the piping bag parallel to the flower nail, place the piping tip at the center of the flower nail, and rotate the nail while simultaneously squeezing the piping bag. Pipe a base about ½" (1.3 cm) in diameter.

3 Starting from the outer perimeter of the base, touch the piping tip against the base and squeeze one leaf onto the base. The curved part of the piping tip should be touching the flower nail while the ends should be pointed upward. Apply pressure to the piping bag as you gently pull it away, gradually releasing pressure while holding the bag at a 10- to 20-degree angle.

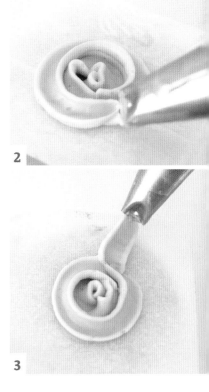

3

4 Shift the piping tip so it's next to the first leaf and repeat step 3, piping elongated leaves around the perimeter of the base.

5 Pipe a second row of leaves on top of the first set, starting slightly inside the first row. As you pipe, release pressure on the piping bag while holding it at a 30- to 40-degree angle. This row will have fewer leaves than the previous one.

6 Pipe a third row of leaves, this time releasing pressure on the bag while holding it at a 50- to 60-degree angle.

7 Once the third layer of leaves is complete, fill in the center with two to four leaves, holding the piping bag at a 70- to 80-degree angle to round out and complete the shape of the agave.

Piping tips: large leaf tip #366 and small round tip #1

Gel color (I used Chefmaster gel color in Super Red and Chefmaster Gold for the centers)

Poinsettia

The showy and unmistakable poinsettia is known for its bold red and green foliage and is most often used in winter and Christmas displays. Although poinsettias are commonly found in red, they can also have light red, pink, or cream foliage. Poinsettias are usually the star of the show, but they also pair wonderfully with other winter elements, such as pine cones (page 76), branches (page 118), and icy sugar snow (page 119).

1   Prepare batches of red and gold buttercreams. Fit one piping bag with the large leaf tip and fill it with red buttercream. Fit another piping bag with the small round tip and fill it with the gold buttercream. With the red buttercream, create a flat, spiral base on a flower nail (see page 41). Hold the piping bag parallel to the flower nail and place the leaf piping tip at the center of the flower nail and rotate the nail while simultaneously squeezing the piping bag. Pipe a base about 1" (2.5 cm) in diameter.

1

2   Starting from the outer perimeter of the base, touch the piping tip against the base and squeeze one petal onto the base. To make sure that the piping tip is oriented correctly, position the piping bag so that the most prominent points of the piping tip are touching the flower nail and top of the spiraled base. Apply pressure to the piping bag as you gently pull it away, gradually releasing pressure while holding it at a 0-degree angle. This allows the petal to lie flat against the flower nail.

3   Move the piping tip next to the first petal and repeat step 2. Continue piping, creating five petals around the perimeter of the base.

4   Pipe a second row of five petals on top of the first set, starting slightly inside the first row. For this row, pipe the petals holding the piping bag at a 10- to 20-degree angle from the flower nail as you release pressure on the bag.

5   Add three more petals in the center, leaving enough room in the center to add the final detail in the next step.

6   To create the center, use the piping bag fitted with the small round tip #1. Pipe a cluster of about seven small pearls of buttercream (see the finished flower, page 91).

Sweet contrasting colors are displayed with mixed botanicals.

No buttercream arrangement is complete without the addition of leaves or foliage. The leaf technique introduces the fourth foundational technique for buttercream botanicals, which allows you to create various types of greenery. The technique can also be adapted to create other buttercream botanicals such as succulents and hellebores.

Leaf I

This first take on a classic leaf is an essential shape that's incredibly versatile. Being creative with the color of these leaves opens enormous possibilities.

Piping tip: small petal tip #103

Gel color (I used Chefmaster Avocado)

1

2

1   Prepare a batch of colored buttercream. Fit a piping bag with the small petal tip and fill it with the buttercream. Place the piping bag so the petal tip is lying almost on its side on the flower nail, with the widest end facing the center of the nail.

2   Squeeze the piping bag and drag the piping tip upward, slightly curving it. Release pressure on the bag and pull the tip away. This should produce a single, curved ribbon.

3   Pipe the other half of the leaf. Start at the top of the ribbon, with the widest end of the tip touching both the flower nail and the first half of the leaf. Follow the curve down to the beginning of the leaf and release pressure to complete the leaf.

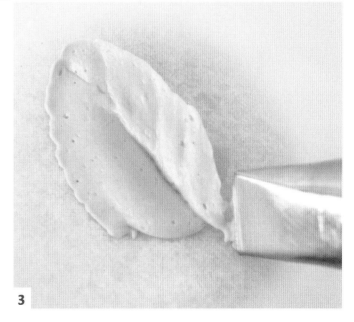

3

Leaf II

This second leaf technique produces a leaf with jagged edges, reminiscent of rose or holly leaves. This type of foliage pairs well with almost any buttercream botanical. Use it with leaf I to add complex texture to your arrangements.

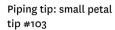

Piping tip: small petal tip #103

Gel color (I used Wilton Moss)

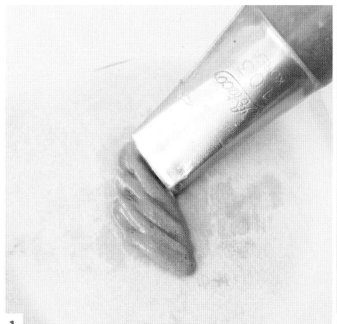

1

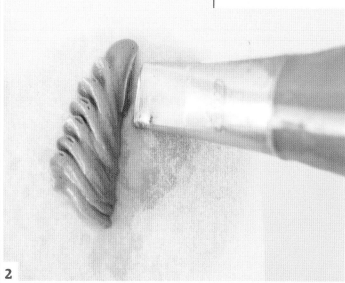

2

3

1   Prepare a batch of colored buttercream. Fit a piping bag with the small petal tip and fill it with the buttercream. Place the piping bag so the petal tip is lying almost on its side on the flower nail, with the widest end facing the center of the nail.

2   Squeeze the piping bag and drag the piping tip upward, slightly curving it and simultaneously zigzagging it.

3   Release pressure on the bag and pull the tip away. This should produce a single rippled ribbon.

4   To create the other half of the leaf, start at the top of the ribbon, positioning the tip so that the widest part is touching both the flower nail and the first half of the leaf. Pipe another ribbon, following the curvature down to the beginning of the leaf using the same zigzag motion. Release pressure on the bag to complete the leaf.

Piping tip: curved petal tip #61

Gel color (I used Americolor in Warm Brown)

Autumn Leaves

Incorporating autumn leaves into a design is a simple way to dramatically change its seasonal aesthetic. Pair these leaves with a grouping of warm-toned botanicals or craft a cascade of autumn leaves in various shades of brown and orange to create a feeling of fall.

1   Prepare a batch of colored buttercream. Fit the piping bag with the curved petal tip and the buttercream. Place the piping bag so the petal tip is lying almost on its side on the flower nail, with the wider end facing the center of the flower nail.

2   Squeeze the piping bag and drag the piping tip upward, creating a slight curve. Release pressure on the bag and pull the tip away. This should produce a single curved ribbon.

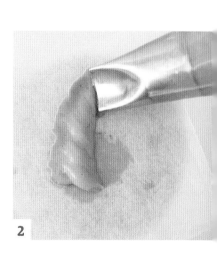

2

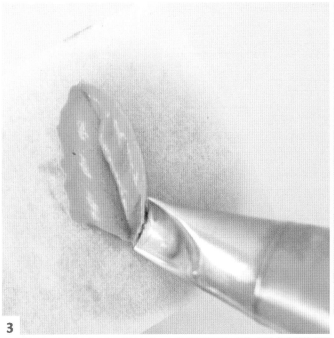

3 For the other half of the leaf, start piping at the top of the ribbon, touching both the flower nail and the first half of the leaf, and then following the curve down to the beginning of the leaf. Release pressure to complete the middle point of the leaf.

4 Repeat steps 2 and 3 and add two slightly smaller leaves piped on each side of the middle leaf.

5 Repeat steps 2, 3, and 4 to add two smaller leaves on either side of the ones just piped to complete the autumn leaf.

Piping tip: curved petal tip #61

Gel color (I used Chefmaster Sky Blue, tinted with a touch of Chefmaster Coal Black)

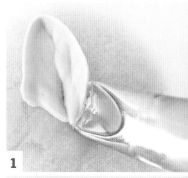

1

2

3

4

Echeveria Succulent III

This lovely plant is created by combining the leaf technique with the blossom technique to produce a botanical with a complex appearance.

1 Prepare a batch of colored buttercream. Fit a piping bag with the curved petal tip and fill the bag with the buttercream. Place the piping bag so the petal tip is lying almost on its side on the flower nail, with the wider end facing the center of the nail. Squeeze the piping bag and drag the piping tip upward with a slight curve, and then release pressure and pull the tip away. This should produce a single curved ribbon.

Pipe the second half of the leaf by starting from the top of the ribbon, touching the flower nail and the first half of the leaf, and then following the curve down to the beginning of the leaf. Release pressure on the bag to complete the main point of the leaf.

2 Repeat steps 1 and 2 to pipe a second leaf next to the first. Repeat the process, piping a total of six leaves, with the last one abutting the first.

3 Pipe another set of leaves on top of the first. The first piped leaf should be between two leaves on the first row. Repeat until you have a complete second set of five or six leaves on top.

4 Tilt the piping bag upright to a 90-degree angle. Pipe a buttercream leaf by gently squeezing the piping bag, then pulling upward to create a short, narrow leaf. Repeat until you have created three to six of these leaves (see the finished plant above).

Piping tips: curved petal tip #120 and small round tip #1

Gel colors (I used Americolor Maroon and Chefmaster Gold)

Hellebore

The hellebore, also known as the Christmas rose, is an uncommon flower with five pointed petals and a wispy stamen. Hellebores bloom in a wide variety of colors that include white and cream, plus varying shades of pinks, reds, purples, almost-black, and even green. Because of the association with Christmas, hellebores can be paired with other wintery botanicals, such as pine cones (page 76). They also work clustered on their own or among other botanicals in any type of arrangement.

1 Prepare batches of maroon and gold buttercreams. Fit a piping bag with the curved petal tip and fill the bag with the maroon buttercream. Fit another bag with the small round tip and fill it with the gold buttercream.

2 Place the piping bag so the petal tip is lying almost on its side on the flower nail, with the wider end facing the center of the nail. Squeeze the piping bag and drag the tip upward, creating a slight curve. Release pressure on the bag and pull the tip away. This should produce a single, curved ribbon.

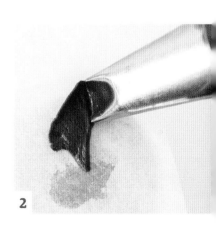

2

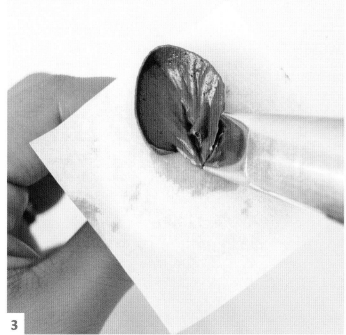

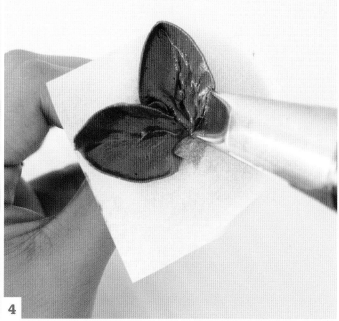

3   Pipe the other half of the petal by starting from the top of the ribbon and following the curve down to the beginning of the petal, touching both the flower nail and the first half of the petal as you go. Release pressure on the bag to complete the petal.

4   Repeat steps 2 and 3 to pipe a second petal next to the first.

5   Repeat the process, piping a total of five petals that abut each other, with the last one next to the first.

6   Using the piping bag fitted with the small round tip, pipe the center of the hellebore. Squeeze several strands of buttercream to fill the center of the flower. Allow the buttercream strands to naturally fall in different directions for a realistic look. The strands should not exceed more than about ¼" (6 mm) in length.

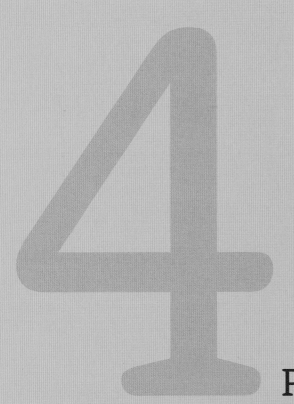

Prepping the Cake Canvas

Now that you've learned the techniques for creating your own beautiful botanicals, you'll need a canvas to display them. That canvas is cake, of course! Whether you display your botanicals on a cupcake or full-size cake, knowing how to prepare this foundation will help you showcase your work. In this chapter, I share my methods for icing a cake and offer a variety of simple ways to add texture and decor to complement your buttercream botanicals. Use these methods individually or combine them to create your own masterpieces.

The Crumb Coat

Creating a crumb coat on a cake before it receives its final icing sets you up for success. A crumb coat is a light buttercream coating spread on the cake's surface. This locks in all those little crumbs that may break free from the surface and become a nuisance during the official icing of the cake.

1   Start with a cake that has been filled. Apply a thin coat of buttercream to the cake with a small metal spatula, being sure to cover the entire surface. You can use an offset or straight spatula, depending on your preference. Chill the cake in the refrigerator for about 5 minutes or until the crumb coating is slightly firm to the touch.

The Icing on the Cake

Once the cake has been crumb coated, it can be formally iced. Before you ice the cake, however, consider the type of finish you want. Although a smooth finish may first come to mind, I'd like to offer other icing possibilities.

Cake turntable

Straight or offset metal spatula, at least 8" (20 cm) long

Cake scraper or straightedge

Smooth Finish

A smooth finish is the most versatile canvas for buttercream botanicals and is often the ideal finish for any cake. Basic white buttercream is never a bad choice, but a pop of color can set a playful tone for a buttercream arrangement. To ice a cake, you'll need the tools listed above. These can be easily found at craft and cake supply stores or online. (For the buttercream recipe, see page 20.)

1   Place a crumb-coated cake (see previous page 20) that's sitting atop a cake board onto the center of the turntable. Centering the cake will ensure the table turns smoothly, allowing for easy smoothing of the icing.

2   Scoop a generous amount of buttercream on top of the cake and smooth it with the spatula, using fluid back-and-forth motions. Rotate the turntable as you spread the icing to help distribute the buttercream evenly on the surface.

2

3

5

6

3   Once the top of the cake appears even, apply buttercream to the sides of the cake. Scrape enough buttercream with the spatula so the flat side of the spatula is covered but not so heavy that the buttercream falls off.

4   Smooth the buttercream on the sides of the cake using fluid back-and-forth motions, evenly distributing the buttercream along the sides. Repeat until the sides of the cake are entirely covered with a layer of buttercream.

5   Place the spatula vertically against the side of the cake. Hold your arm and spatula steady while you gradually spin the turntable. This distributes the buttercream more evenly.

6   Finish the sides with the cake scraper. Hold the scraper against the cake, making sure the bottom edge of the scraper is flat against the cake board. Be sure to use a cake scraper that is at least the full height of your cake or taller as a scraper that's too short may add unwanted lines on the surface. Slowly rotate the turntable as you hold the cake scraper steady. This process will scrape off some of the buttercream while smoothing out the surface.

8

7 Remove any excess buttercream from the cake scraper and continue rotating the turntable until the sides of the cake are fully smooth.

8 As in step 7, remove any excess buttercream from the cake scraper. Turn the cake scraper horizontally. Glide it along the top edge of the cake to remove any excess buttercream, creating a flat top. Rotate the cake and smooth the top with the cake scraper to remove excess icing.

9 Rotate the turntable to reposition the cake and repeat step 8 until the top is flat and smooth.

Colored Icings

Smooth icing doesn't necessarily mean plain. Smooth icings in vivid colors can completely change the tone of a design from soft and elegant to bold, playful, and unexpected.

When creating a vibrant or saturated icing color, it's likely you'll use a larger quantity of gel color to achieve the desired shade. Be sure to taste the colored icing before icing your cake. Sometimes adding copious amounts of gel color can cause the taste of the icing to change, adding an unpleasant bitterness, reminiscent of iodine. Saturated colors such as reds, pinks, purples, and blacks can be especially problematic and can leave a bitter taste. Be sure to sample the buttercream as the color develops to gauge any shift in flavor. To correct an altered or bitter taste, add some uncolored buttercream. This will desaturate the color to a degree but will make the buttercream much more palatable.

Rustic Textures

A rustic texture is a fantastic option for the first-time cake icer or for days when creating a perfectly smooth finish feels too demanding. Rustic textures, created with a small metal spatula, lend a vintage artisan aesthetic to a cake.

1 Follow steps 1 through 6 of the Smooth Finish technique (see pages 105 to 107).

FOR A HORIZONTAL TEXTURE

1 Hold a small metal spatula horizontally and position it at the base of the iced cake. Rotate the turntable while holding the spatula steady to create an indent around the perimeter of the cake.

2 Once the cake has made a full rotation and the spatula is at the starting point, slowly slide the spatula horizontally away from the cake surface and reposition it just above the first indent.

3 Repeat steps 1 and 2, working your way up the sides of the cake until you reach the top edge.

FOR A VERTICAL TEXTURE

1 Hold a small metal spatula vertically and position it at the base of the iced cake.

2 Using a slow, upward stroke, glide the spatula along the surface of the cake until you reach the top edge.

3 Reposition the spatula at the base, next to the first indent, and repeat the process until you've created the texture all the way around the cake.

FOR A DIAGONAL TEXTURE

1 For this technique you'll need a small metal spatula with a narrow tip. Place the spatula at the base of the iced cake, holding it at a diagonal.

2 Using a slow, upward stroke, glide the spatula along the surface of the cake until you reach the top edge (**a**). Reposition the spatula at the base, next to the first indent, and repeat the process until you've created the texture around the sides of the cake (**b**).

Piped Textures

Inspired by textiles, these piped textures elevate the look of a cake. Simple, repetitive piping motions and, in some cases, playful use of color, create gorgeous patterns that imitate woven or embroidered fabric.

Use metal or plastic cookie cutters to imprint shapes as a guide on the sides of the cake. You can also use a scribe tool (a sharp, pointy needlelike tool used to scratch designs into buttercream) or toothpick to create an outline to guide the piped buttercream designs.

Scribe tool or toothpick

Piping tip: small round #1

Buttercream, any color

Second shade of buttercream for accents (optional)

Stitch Piping

This stitch technique is an introduction to embroidery-style piping. Delicate stitching along the sides of your cake lends a charming and handmade quality to the overall decor. Stitched patterns can be displayed throughout the surface of your canvas for an intricate pattern, or they can be piped strategically for an extra touch of decor.

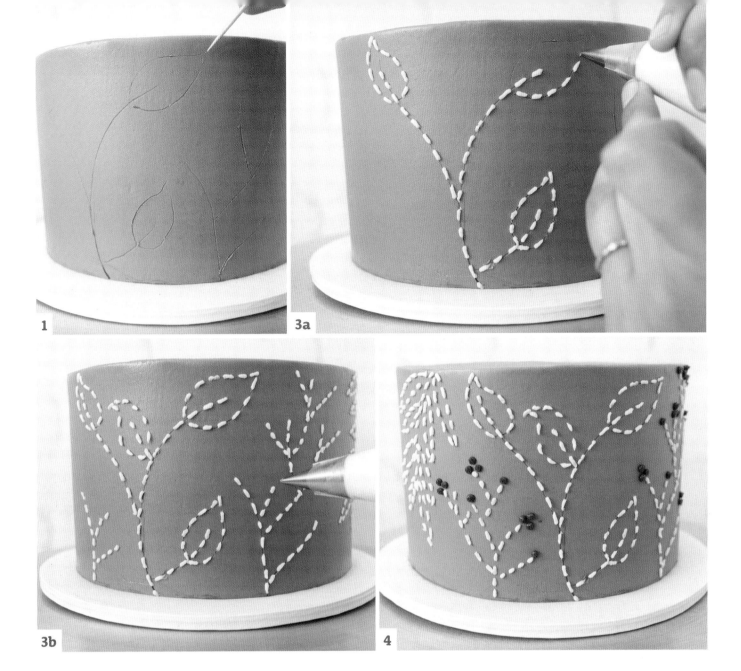

1   Begin with a cake iced with a smooth finish
(see pages 105 to 107). Make sure the surface is
completely smooth; a rough or bumpy surface
will cause the piped detail to sit unevenly on the
cake surface. Using a scribe tool or toothpick,
gently graze the point along the surface of the
cake, creating the outline of the desired pattern.
I created a freehand leaf and stem pattern for an
organic look. Be careful not to gouge the sides
of the cake as you create the design. If a more
uniform pattern is desired, opt for fondant leaf- or
paisley-shaped cutters. Gently press the cutter
against the side of the cake surface and carefully
pull away to reveal the design.

2   Fit a piping bag with the small round tip and fill it
with the shade of buttercream you've chosen for
the stitches. Following the pattern, squeeze the
bag and deposit a short line of buttercream to
resemble a stitch.

3   Follow the outline, creating evenly spaced lines of
buttercream until the pattern is complete (**a** and **b**).

4   *Optional:* Fit another piping bag with a small round
tip and fill it with another shade of buttercream.
Add a few small buttercream dots at the tips of
some of the piped stems. This is a great way to
break up the pattern and add a touch of color.

Embroidery Piping

Embroidery piping adds bold and eclectic texture to your canvas. Choose a series of strong colors for a festive look or soft, muted colors for a more subtle approach.

Round cookie cutter, 1½" and 1" (4 and 2.5 cm) diameter

Piping tips: one round tip #1 per color used

Gel colors (Choose a bold or distinctive palette with a minimum of three colors. Here, I used a total of eight vibrant colors.)

1 Touch the sides of the cake with the 1½" (4 cm) round cutter to create imprinted circular outlines. Stagger the circles and space them evenly around the cake, making sure to leave space for smaller circles.

2 Fill in the empty spaces with smaller circular outlines using the 1" (2.5 cm) round cutter.

3 Fit several piping bags with small round tips and fill them with your chosen colors. Pipe a small circle in the center of one of the 1½" (4 cm) circle outlines.

4 Using a side-to-side motion, pipe horizontal strands of buttercream starting from the top of the circle and working your way around until the circle has been filled in.

5 Choose another color of buttercream. Starting just outside the center circle, pipe buttercream strands that go from the outer edge of the center circle to about halfway into the circular outline, creating a zigzag pattern. The design should look like a flower or starburst. Repeat the pattern once or twice more using different colors, following the outer perimeter of each piped circle until the initial outline has been filled.

6 Repeat steps 3 through 6 to fill in the remaining circular outlines, using a variety of colors.

7 *Optional:* Add small dots of buttercream (I used white) around the embroidered appliqués to add texture and balance the distribution of color.

5

Adding Final Touches and Creating Arrangements

Creating botanical arrangements on a cake and adding final touches bring all the elements together to create stunning showpieces. Buttercream botanicals such as flowers and succulents are stunning focal points of any arrangement, but adding accents (known as fillers), such as flower buds, branches, and simple leaves, can amplify a composition. Fillers allow an arrangement to be more balanced. They fill in empty spaces, add color, and help a grouping take shape. Designing an arrangement of buttercream botanicals is perhaps the most satisfying part of the creation process. Putting an arrangement together allows you to let your creativity flow and your inner floral designer shine. Over the years, I've developed many tips and tricks for creating cohesive, attractive groupings using a variety of botanicals, and I share them with you in this chapter.

Botanical Filler Elements

This series of botanical filler elements provides some simple ways to add realistic details with minimal effort. Botanical elements are piped details that include flower buds, foliage, and branches. They can be used both to fill gaps or define the shape of your arrangement.

Piping tip: leaf tip #352

Gel color (I used Chefmaster Avocado)

Easy Leaves

Unlike the leaves featured in chapter 3, The Leaf Technique (see pages 94 to 101), these leaves are much simpler, easier to produce, and require little effort. They can be piped in at the last minute to fill in spaces within any size arrangement on cakes and cupcakes. They also help break up dense clustering of color to provide balance.

1   Prepare a batch of colored buttercream. Fit a piping bag with the leaf tip and fill it with the buttercream. Choose the area to which you'd like to add leaves and insert the piping tip into that space.

2   Squeeze the piping bag and gradually pull the tip away, releasing pressure to produce a single pointed leaf. Create more leaves as desired.

1

2a

2b

Flower Buds

For a charming addition of color and texture, enter flower buds. Buds add realism and an organic feel to any arrangement as they resemble not-yet-opened flowers. These round buds are the perfect space filler to complement any flower.

1   Prepare a batch of green and burgundy buttercreams. Fit one piping bag with the #8 piping tip and fill it with the buttercream for the green buds, and fit the other bag with the #6 tip and fill it with the burgundy buttercream for the flower buds. Locate the gaps within the arrangement for placement of the flower buds. Using the #8 tip, pipe a round pearl of buttercream.

2   Using the #6 tip, touch the tip of the pearl you just created and gently insert the end of the piping tip (**a**). Pipe a second, smaller pearl inside the first. The first pearl will slightly expand to expose the color of the bud (**b**).

tip | For a realistic look to flower buds, distribute them as single buds and in clusters of two or three.

1

Gel color (I used
Chefmaster Buckeye
Brown with a touch of
Chefmaster Coal
Black to create a
blackish-brown)

2

Branches

Piped tree branches add movement and shape to botanical displays. They can extend
the shape of an arrangement and fill in an empty surface, making them ideal for cakes.
Branches can also give buttercream designs a rustic and woodsy feel.

1 Prepare a batch of colored buttercream.
Fit a piping bag with the #4 tip and
fill it with the buttercream. Pipe
lines extending from the botanical
arrangement. Hold the piping bag
about ¼" (6 mm) above the cake
surface and squeeze the bag to allow
the line of buttercream to drop and fall
into place. For the first branch, pipe
one line starting from the edge of the
buttercream botanical arrangement and

extending about 3" (7.5 cm) or more,
depending on how much space you'd
like to fill. For these branches, straight
lines are discouraged and imperfections
are encouraged to add a touch of realism.

2 Add shorter branches to the main
buttercream lines and smaller, finer
branch accents.

tip For arrangements on
top of a cake sur-
face, allow the outer
branches to follow
the curvature of
the top of the cake,
and then fill in with
smaller branches.

Other Filler Elements

Nonpareil Sprinkles

These tiny white sprinkles are often my secret weapon for adding texture, balance, and contrast to my arrangements. White nonpareils are my go-to addition for botanical arrangements that need a little something extra.

1 To add nonpareils to a grouping of botanicals, take a small amount of sprinkles between your thumb and index finger and move your fingers back and forth to let the sprinkles fall in the desired area (they stick best on freshly piped buttercream). Here, they resemble baby's breath.

> ¼ cup (50 g) granulated sugar
>
> ¼ cup (50 g) coarse crystal or sanding sugar
>
> Approximately 2 teaspoons (10 ml) water

Icy Sugar Snow

This easy recipe for icy sugar snow can be stored indefinitely and added to any winter- or holiday-themed arrangement. Using two textures or different size granules is key to getting the perfect look of icy snow clusters.

1 Combine the sugars in a bowl or container.

2 Add the water. Mix the sugars and water until the sugar crystals are moist enough to form a coarse consistency with some clumps. If no clumps form, add a third teaspoon or more of water until the sugar binds together and clumps form.

3 Empty the mixture onto a parchment paper–lined tray. Spread the sugar unevenly, encouraging clumps in various sizes to form. Allow to dry for several hours or overnight in a dry area. Store the snow in a lidded container.

Selecting Botanical Elements for Arrangements

When selecting buttercream botanical elements for my arrangements, I first consider my desired aesthetic. For arrangements with a romantic feel, I often choose botanicals with lots of ruffles and volume, such as peonies and roses, and opt for a soft color palette of creams or neutrals with hints of soft peach and blush. For complex designs with lots of color and texture, I go for a bold color palette and choose a wide variety of botanicals. Whatever aesthetic you choose, these simple guidelines will help you achieve a balanced arrangement.

- **Select at least three elements for a well-balanced grouping.** Begin by choosing at least one botanical variety to be the main element, then choose two more elements to support the main element. Leaves and fillers can be considered elements. For an arrangement of classic roses, for example, the roses would be the main element, and the other two elements could be leaves and baby's breath. Alternatively, roses with two different varieties of leaves would also work.

- **Variety is key.** Choose a selection of elements that vary in color, texture, and/or size. Too much of one element within an arrangement, such as a bouquet of one color and size of dahlia, can make it difficult to determine where one flower ends and another begins. Adding variety with color or size or including other botanical elements creates definition and is more pleasing to the eye.

- **When using a diverse color palette, distribute the boldest colors evenly throughout the arrangement,** either as single botanicals or as clusters. The most vivid colors draw the eye first, so distributing them evenly creates balance. Fill in spaces with lighter colors.

- **Don't forget the greenery.** Including leaves or green elements adds a defining quality to arrangements. Greens break up the color palette and alleviate any heaviness.

- **Extras such as flower buds, baby's breath, and branches are optional** (see pages 116 to 119), but they're attractive and provide simple ways to fill in unwanted gaps and create a nice flow that helps shape your buttercream arrangements.

Preparation

Before arranging any botanical buttercreams on a cake or cupcake, make sure they've been piped and are frozen. Freezing botanicals helps them keep their shape as you handle and arrange them. Because my buttercream recipe is not a crusting buttercream, freezing is a necessary step. American-style buttercreams often contain shortening and a large ratio of sugar, giving them a firm consistency. When sitting at room temperature for a period of time, they develop a firm crust on the exterior. However, my buttercream recipe doesn't contain any shortening, and the ratio of sugar is much less than American-style buttercream. The consistency is softer and easier to pipe, and the buttercream stays soft and malleable at room temperature. Frozen botanicals should feel cold and solid to the touch. If your finger leaves an indent, continue to freeze until they're hard. Usually 20 minutes in the freezer is the minimum amount of time for botanicals to solidify enough for handling.

Prepare your canvas of choice (see chapter 4, page 104). I used an 8-inch (20 cm) round cake iced in white buttercream. You can go in any direction with your canvas, such as rustic and simplistic or bold and intricate. As I mentioned earlier, I like to think about the overall aesthetic of the cake before I prepare the canvas. I usually keep my canvas simple to allow the buttercream botanicals to take center stage, choosing white, cream, or a muted shade of icing with a smooth or textured finish. For occasions that call for a statement look, I opt for bold color. Make sure your cake is iced and chilled before you begin creating your arrangement.

tip | If your workspace is warmer than 75°F (24°C), the botanicals will thaw more rapidly. In this case, remove the botanicals from the freezer in batches, and try to work more quickly. You can always return a tray of piped botanicals to the freezer for a few minutes to allow them to rechill.

Think about the general form your arrangement will take, such as a semicircle or complete circle around the cake top. Then, pipe a mound, or platform, of room-temperature buttercream in roughly the shape of the composition.

For a crescent-shaped arrangement, for example, use a piping bag with a wide-snipped opening (no piping tip needed) and pipe a platform of room-temperature buttercream in a crescent shape. This mound should be wide and tall at the center and tapered at both ends. The overall size of the platform should match the size of your arrangement. The platform serves three purposes:

1. It provides a template to help you visualize where the botanicals will be placed.

2. It provides a platform for the botanicals that gives the arrangement volume and dimension.

3. It acts as glue for adhering the chilled botanicals to the cake canvas.

Once the buttercream platform has been piped, remove the trays of botanicals from the freezer. As they sit at room temperature (ideally 68°F to 75°F [20°C to 24°C]), they'll begin to defrost and soften, so it's best to work quickly.

Creating an Arrangement

Once you have selected your botanical elements and prepared your canvas, you are ready to complete your design. Whether you choose to create a crescent-shaped arrangement, a bouquet, or a wreath, follow these simple steps to achieve your beautifully designed botanical arrangement.

1 Carefully peel the parchment paper away from each botanical piece and place the piece on the desired area on the cake or cupcake.

2 Determine the focal point of the arrangement and place the key botanicals there. Work your way out as you place the other pieces. For this crescent-shaped grouping of roses,

I placed the largest flowers in the center of the crescent (the widest part) and worked outward toward the tapered ends. If you have a few varieties of botanicals in various sizes, place the largest pieces first and then fill in with smaller ones, placing some of the smaller botanicals at the ends to finish the arrangement.

3   Gently secure the piece in place by applying enough pressure to the lower sides of the botanical to attach it to the buttercream mound, being careful not to break the petals or leaves. Wearing gloves and using a small offset metal spatula to help secure the botanicals can be helpful. Repeat with the remaining botanicals to build the arrangement.

4   Leaves and other optional fillers (see chapter 5, page 114) should be placed last as the finishing touches of your arrangement. Once the pieces are arranged, the cake should be refrigerated to further secure them in place.

This arrangement may look complex, but when broken down into steps, it's quite simple to create. Thinking and planning ahead goes a long way in creating a cohesive composition. This grouping includes one type of flower, the classic rose, but when piped in different colors, it adds a wow factor to the cake.

Resources

Online cake decorating supplies and equipment:
- BakeDeco/Kerekes: bakedeco.com
- NY Cake: nycake.com

Specialty piping tips and tools:
- Blooms by June: bloomsbyjune.square.site
- Suzy's Sweet Tooth: suzyssweettooth.com

Acknowledgments

To my little family, Daniel and Magnolia: You both are my constant motivation and source of strength. Family hugs and "You can do it, Mommy" were all I needed some days. I hope I make you both proud.

To my mama: Who knew that a cake decorating class you took when I was a kid would inspire my career? Not us, but I am forever grateful for it. Thank you for letting me check out too many baking books from the library and for teaching me how to use the real oven since the light-bulb in the Easy-Bake Oven wasn't enough to bake a real cake.

To Maggie and Lito, the best mother- and father-in-law anyone could ask for: Thank you for making Noli part of your weekly routine and making memories with her while I work.

To my students all over the world: Thank you for your love and support throughout the years. This book was made with all of you in mind.

To every friend and family member who believed in me, sometimes even more than I believed in myself: This is for you.

And a big thank-you to the **team at Quarto** for making this book possible.

About the Author

Leslie Vigil is a world-renowned cake artist known for creating cake art almost exclusively in buttercream. A graduate of Le Cordon Bleu culinary school with an emphasis on baking and patisserie, she has more than a decade of experience in the cake industry in both professional bakery and home settings. Leslie shares her years of knowledge with her students, demonstrating how seemingly complicated methods can be simplified and achievable for almost anyone of any skill level.

A self-proclaimed "flour child" and buttercream enthusiast, Leslie creates edible art inspired by nature and floral design, with influences from her Mexican heritage. Leslie uses buttercream as her preferred medium for her cake art, which includes realistic floral bouquets and potted cacti in terracotta vessels. Leslie teaches students via online classes and in-person workshops, where she showcases the versatility of buttercream. Leslie is thrilled to share her four foundational buttercream techniques, her signature recipe for buttercream, and her approachable method for making sophisticated floral cake designs so everyone can create their own beautiful buttercream botanicals.

Index

Index